SRI GURU GRANTH SAHIB DISCOVERED

SRI
GURU GRANTH SAHIB
DISCOVERED

A Reference Book of Quotations
from the Adi Granth
selected by

HAKIM SINGH RAHI

MOTILAL BANARSIDASS PUBLISHERS
PRIVATE LIMITED ● DELHI

First Edition: Delhi, 1999

ISBN: 81-208-1613-7

Also available at:

MOTILAL BANARSIDASS

41 U.A. Bungalow Road, Jawahar Nagar, Delhi 110 007
8 Mahalaxmi Chamber, Warden Road, Mumbai 400 026
120 Royapettah High Road, Mylapore, Chennai 600 004
Sanas Plaza, 1302, Baji Rao Road, Pune 411 002
16 St. Mark's Road, Bangalore 560 001
8 Camac Street, Calcutta 700 017
Ashok Rajpath, Patna 800 004
Chowk, Varanasi 221 001

FOR SALE IN U.K. ONLY

Distributed in U.K. by
Pippa Rann Books, PO Box 43, Sutton, Surrey, SM2 5WL.

PRINTED IN INDIA
BY JAINENDRA PRAKASH JAIN AT SHRI JAINENDRA PRESS,
A-45 NARAINA, PHASE I, NEW DELHI 110 028
AND PUBLISHED BY NARENDRA PRAKASH JAIN FOR
MOTILAL BANARSIDASS PUBLISHERS PRIVATE LIMITED,
BUNGALOW ROAD, DELHI 110 007

FOREWORD

Sikhism is a distinct religion, not an offshoot of Hinduism or a synthesis of Hinduism and Islam, selecting the best of both religions. There are still books which present both these interpretations of Sikhism and readers are warned against them. Many Hindus regard the other faiths which have arisen in India, Buddhism and Sikhism for example, as part of the diversity which is essentially Hindu. Those who support the syncretist view usually mean that Sikhism conforms to their own image of what is good, for example, the rejection of caste, or the stress on monotheism, appear wholesome to Christians and are found in Islam.

Sikhism has its own institutions and, in particular, a scripture which it considers to be a result of divine revelation and to be the inspired Word of God.

The Guru Granth Sahib, known as the Adi Granth until Guru Gobind Singh conferred guruship upon it in 1708 as he was dying, is the product of six of the ten Gurus. It is remarkable for the fact that it includes compositions by men who were not Sikhs, such people as Kabir, or the Muslim Sufi mystic, Sheikh Farid. Hakim Singh Rahi does not include any of their compositions in his analysis and in some ways this is a pity, because, to my knowledge, there is no other world scripture which contains the words of men or women who were not members of the religion. However, these mystics add little or nothing to the message delivered by the Gurus and for this reason, their omission is justified. The task which the author set himself was enormous enough without expanding it.

The importance of the Guru Granth Sahib becomes obvious immediately when one enters the prayer hall (diwan) of a gurdwara. It is to be seen as the focal point of worship, placed on a dais, resting on cushions and under a canopy. It looks like an enthroned emperor and that, in a sense, is what it is, for it is the living Word of God, not a mere Book. (Notice the capitalising of the "B" which many Sikhs use). As they enter the place of worship, the gurdwara, some will bow low and touch the steps with their right hand which they will then place to their forehead. They are applying the dust of the "sainst", members of the congregation, or sangat. By this gesture they are recognising their indebtedness to their fellow Sikhs and the presence of God in the sangat. Sikhism is a congregational religion, each Sikh is a member of the family of God. As they come into the scripture's presence they will kneel or even prostrate themselves, expressing respect and intended obedience to the divine Word. Some observers have suggested that they are worshipping the Book. They are clearly wrong, what is being worshipped is all that it represents.

Guru Nanak's mission and message were simple. He was summoned by God to bring men and women to true devotion, something that was being neglected in favour of ritualism. When he was about thirty years old, in 1599 the young Nanak, already noted for his piety underwent a transforming experience which he later described as being taken to God's court. His words in the Adi Granth read:

> I was a minstrel out of work,
> The Lord gave me employment.
> The mighty one instructed me,
> "Night and day, sing my praise".
> The Lord summoned the minstrel
> To his high court.
> On me he bestowed the robe of honouring
> Him and singing his praise.
>
> On me he bestowed the nectar in a cup,
> The nectar of his true and holy Name,
> Those who at the feet of the Guru
> Feast and take their fill of the Lord's holiness
> Attain peace and joy.
> Your minstrel spreads your glory
> By singing your word.
> Nanak (says), through adoring the truth
> We attain to the all-highest. (Adi Granth page 150)

From this time Nanak is known as Guru Nanak. A Guru is someone who is conscious of being called by God not only to receive spiritual liberation but to bring it to others. His message was summed up in the words: "Na koi Hindu, na koi Mussalman," ("there is no Hindu, there is no Muslim"). He went on to ask, "Whose path (teaching) shall I follow? I will follow God's path. He is neither Hindu nor Muslim."

Perhaps a comment needs to be provided on Guru Nanak's attitude to the other expressions of religion which he encountered, Hinduism, Islam and forms of yoga in particular. It is in the context of Guru Nanak's calling and mission that his attitude to Hinduism, Islam and also such matters as vegetarianism and even the disposal of the dead must be understood. What he saw around him were distortions which obscured the message of liberation. At Haridwar, a town on the Ganges in northern India, he came across people offering water to the sun as part of their devotions. He began to throw water in the direction of Punjab. That was where his fields were, and if the water of the pilgrims could reach the sun which was millions of miles away, he could irrigate his fields in the same way! Again, in his village, he was one day visiting its Muslim headman and a religious leader who happened to be with him. At the time of prayer they invited him to join them. Afterwards, they accused him of not taking part. The Guru said he could not. They had not been praying, their minds were on worldly matters. One was worrying whether his horse had fallen down the well in the courtyard. The other was wondering what price the horses he had sent to the market were fetching! On another occasion he came across a yogi who claimed to be able to tell the future while in a trance. The Guru removed the bowl which was in front of him. When he opened his eyes the yogi demanded to know who had taken it. The Guru expressed surprise that someone with powers to foretell did not know what had become of his dish! Vegetarianism is often associated with ritual pollution, being defiled by what is eaten. Guru Nanak said the only pollutant was moral. As for arguing over the issues of cremation or inhumation, the Guru said that what should be of concern was the destiny of the soul after death. If it did not find its home with God, whatever happened was bad news!

Liberation here and now as the result of human yearning and, above all God's grace, was and is the message of Sikhism. It was available for everyone, rich or poor, male or female, of whatever caste or human division or sect. In God's presence all were and are equal. That is why, in a gurdwara, everyone sits on the floor and is required to partake of a meal called langar, which is vegetarian, so that no one need feel unable to share in it. God, who is beyond the categories of male and female, though personal in the sense that the divine attributes are love, mercy, and compassion, and a concern for justice, for example, has no favourites or gender bias. (In Punjabi there is no neuter case so Manmohan Singh, and following him, the present author, have had recourse to the use of male epithets, though, of course, to describe God as "it" would have anyway been inappropriate).

Mr Rahi has done a great service to Sikhs and English readers who are not Sikh by providing them with this book but if they are to benefit from it one requirement must be observed; they must be humble.

A famous Christian, Canon Max Warren, wrote in the nineteen fifties:

> "Our first task in approaching another people, another culture, another
> religion is to take off our shoes, for the ground we are approaching

is holy. Else we may find ourselves treading on men's dreams. More serious still, we may forget that god was here before our arrival. We have, then to ask what is the authentic religious content of the experience of the Muslim, the Hindu, the Buddhist, or whoever he may be... We have, in a word, to be 'present' with them."

As someone else, a native American, put it: until you have travelled in someone else's moccasins for a mile you should not judge him.

We must be prepared to listen, something that westerners in particular, are not always noted for! As we come to the extracts which make up this book we must recognise that we are reading what Sikhs believe to be the Word of God. I share this belief, though I am not a Sikh. Other readers who may not do so are requested to take off their shoes, that is their cultural baggage, and listen. Otherwise what they will gain from their reading will be of limited value. Some readers may wish to be critical. That is the first reaction of some to whatever others have done. "I could do better," may often be said by those who have done nothing at all! It would be very difficult for anyone to improve on Hakim Singh Rahi's work.

The wish to rush into making comparisons between Sikhism and other religions is also one to be discouraged. Much better to be enriched by the sustenance provided. Using this kind of analogy the fifth teacher, Guru Arjan, when he had completed the first compilation of the Adi Granth wrote:

> "In the platter are placed three things, truth, contentment, and meditation. The Nectar-Name of the Lord, who is the support of all, has also been put therein. If someone partakes of this fare, if someone relishes it, he (or she) is emancipated."
>
> (Adi Granth, p. 1429)

Of course the Guru uttered poems many stanzas long, as well as shorter pieces which were only couplets. Some Sikhs, therefore, have been critical of providing extracts, but there is a long history of such anthologies, the most notable being the UNESCO compilation of 1960, *The Sacred Writings of the Sikhs*. It is still a popular and valuable collection, and in my early years of studying Sikhism, I relied heavily upon it. However, it was not thematic, as the present volume is, and it was much more limited in content.

I can see Mr Rahi's work helping Sikhs, especially those involved in interfaith discussions, teachers of GCSE and A level pupils (in the British system, or Class/Grade 10-12), non-Sikhs who wish to learn what the Gurus taught about many aspects of Sikh philosophy (a word often preferred to theology), and undergraduates encountering the religion for the first time. Each section is carefully and reliably introduced by the book's author who clearly understands the religion well.

In commending *Sri Guru Granth Sahib Discovered* perhaps I may be allowed to make two further points, one is to the author, namely that a similar volume needs to be written on the Gurus' teachings on social and ethical issues. If he is not too exhausted that might be his next act of seva (voluntary service, not only to Sikhs but to humanity in general). The second is to the Shromani Gurdwara Parbandhak Committee, whose authorised version has been the source of the author's quotations. It is that Manmohan Singh's monumental work is thirty years old and more (the first volume appeared in 1962). Just as the King James version of the Bible has been augmented by many others, to meet the needs of people for whom its English is difficult to understand, so there is a requirement, especially for Sikhs growing up in the English speaking parts of the diaspora for a similar modern translation. Sadly, for many of them Punjabi, and its written form, gurmukhi, is almost a foreign language. The Gurus used the language of the day, not Sanskrit, so that the Word which they received could be handed on as effectively as possible; so I would want to argue, modern English, French, or translations in other languages would be no more than the fulfilment of the Guru's mission to spread God's glory throughout the world.

However, this introduction and commendation must end on the positive note which it deserves. Mr Rahi has tried to ensure that his book will be as user-friendly to them as possible. English speaking Sikhs who use it will certainly be able to meet the eternal Sat Guru in its pages.

Dr W Owen Cole
Chichester Institute of Higher Education, Chichester, England
August 1998

ACKNOWLEDGEMENTS

Let me begin by thanking Mr. Rahmat Jagirdar of Handsworth, Birmingham, who was a real source of inspiration in undertaking this difficult work. He very graciously provided me with six volumes of the Sri Guru Granth Sahib, translated by the late Sri Manmohan Singh, in order to start my work on this book. My thanks are also due to Mr. Taj. M. Bhatti.

By March 1996 Revd. Basil Scott, my kind and good friend, had paid me several visits and had come to know about this project, which I had been working on for several years. By that time, I had almost completed the work on the six volumes and had gathered copious pages of material. I had known Revd. and Mrs. Basil Scott from India, and had often worked with him. He was excited about the need and prospects for the book and the purpose it was going to serve. He very kindly offered me his kind support and invited me to his house in Derby, to stay with him and his dear wife Shirley, to complete this project undisturbed and away from home. His kind offer, I gratefully accepted and started work on the book at his home, enjoying his hospitality.

Then came the need to secure the last two volumes of Manmohan Singh's translation of the Granth. He very kindly secured the seventh volume for me through one of his friends in London.

In the meantime Mr. Taj Bhatti's dear wife Rani visitied India and she very kindly brought the last two volumes from Amritsar. I am very grateful to her for her timely help. This enabled me to continue the work on the Granth and to collect more selections from these volumes.

After this came the mammoth task of arranging and re-arranging, sifting and editing the material, which was very graciously undertaken by Basil Scott with his wide experience and expertise in this field. This book would never had seen the press if it were not for his efforts. I am equally indebted to his dear wife Shirley for her Christian care and rich hospitality and great help from time to time in correcting and re-writing certain passages of the book. I therefore, proudly dedicate this book to Basil and Shirley Scott for their unselfish love and care.

Sincere thanks also go to Greta Weller, Rosie Scott and Christine Sond for all their skill and hard work in typing the manuscript.

Hakim Singh Rahi

CONTENTS

SALVATION ACCORDING TO SHRI GURU GRANTH SAHIB

GOD
SACH KHAND

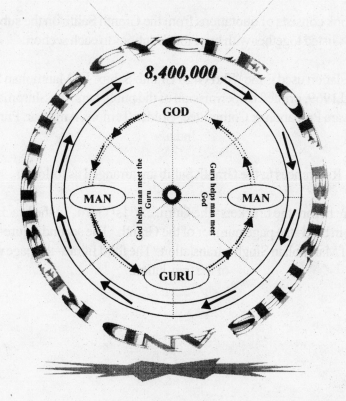

This diagram shows the path of salvation from the relentless cycle of birth and rebirth. On the basis of past deeds (karma), God writes each person's destiny at birth. Where destiny is favourable, God causes some to meet the Guru. The Guru by his grace grants the Name (Name) to the fortunate, who by meditating on the Name according to the Guru's instructions obtain the vision of God.

(The front cover design by Raj Sahota is based on the cycle of births and rebirths diagram)

This book consists of quotations from the Granth Sahib on the subjects
listed together with brief introductions to each section.

The translation used is the "Shri Guru Granth Sahib" by Manmohan Singh,
dated 1969, printed by permission of the publishers, the Shiromani
Gurdwara Prabandhak Committee, Golden Temple, Amritsar, Punjab,
India.

References to the Granth Sahib are arranged as follows:

The figure before the brackets=the Guru, e.g. 1st Guru. In the brackets the
figure in bold=the page number of the Granth. The second figure=the
volume of Manmohan Singh's translation. The third figure=the page number
of the translation.

1

ORIGINS OF THE GRANTH

1. What is the Sri Guru Granth Sahib?

The Sri Guru Granth Sahib is the Holy Book, or scriptures, of the Sikh people, who originate from the area of Punjab in north India. It contains material from the period of the Sikh Gurus, 1469 - 1708 A.D. It was written in Gurmukhi, which draws on the riches of both the Sanskrit and Persian languages and their derivations.

It is a voluminous book of 1430 pages. The book was first compiled by the 5th Guru, Guru Arjan, in 1603-4. This contains hymns written by the first 5 gurus and is known as the Adi-Granth. It also contains hymns by other great saints from Hindu and Muslim backgrounds, such as Sant Kabir, Nam Dev, Ravi Das and Farid. Later, the 10th Guru, Guru Govind Singh re-edited this Adi Granth, added newer compositions and re-issued it in a definitive form.

Dr. Gopal Singh writes: "The tenth Guru, Govind Singh, re-edited the Adi-Granth, and fixed its form finally in the form in which we find it today, expunging apocryphal writings, amending a few spellings, adding 4 hymns in the beginning for evening prayers but not adding any of his own compositions, except perhaps one couplet ascribed to him and leaving the Granth as it was before in the days of Guru Arjan."[1]

Its hymns are written in couplets of differing metres and are set to various tunes (*ragas*). They are intended for use on specific occasions, seasons, months, days or times of day. They are prayers of praise and adoration of Almighty God (W*ahe-guru*), the Eternal One (A*kaal purukh*). The hymns are relevant to almost all people, whatever their place in society, at whatever stage in their lives. They are designed to be

---

Sri Guru Granth Sahib. Translated and annotated by Dr. Gopal Singh. World Sikh University Press, 1978, Introduction, Vol.1, p. xlvii.

accompanied musically by singers (*ragis*), who sing regularly in the temples (*gurdwaras*) or in the homes of members on auspicious occasions. A regular ceremony is the *akhand-paath*, when the entire Sri Guru Granth Sahib is read or recited continuously from beginning to end. This takes 48 hours to perform.

Sikh people have a very high regard indeed for this book and it can be said that they almost worship it as the living embodiment of God. It is always placed on a high platform in the temple and is kept wrapped in clean and costly cloths, which are changed periodically. Holy water is sprinkled on and around it, to purify the place. A fan called a *chawri* is waved over it to keep flies away while recitals or readings are in progress. At night the holy Granth is put to rest.

When the tenth Guru lay dying and was asked who the next Guru was to be, he said: "The word is the spiritual Guru as contained in the Adi-Granth. The secular Guru is the *panth* or the whole *khalsa* in faith."[2]

Gurbani

The Granth is called Gurbani meaning the word of the Guru. The Granth is also called Dhurbani (direct word from God) and the abode of the trans-cendental Lord, thus making it the embodiment of God, although the majority of the Granth consists of the personal praise and prayers of the Gurus to the creator God.

3rd Guru: The exalted Guru's word is God Himself and it is through his word that man obtains union with God.
3rd (**39**/1/132)

1st Guru: He Himself understands the mental outlook of all. Nanak, the Lord Himself has uttered forth the word.
Ist (**150**/I/503)

3rd Guru: Some rare ones realise by the Guru's grace that the Lord is contained in the Guru's word.
3rd (**1332-3**/8/4398)

5th Guru: This holy book (Adi Granth) is the abode of the transcendent Lord.
5th (**1226**/7/4039)

1st Guru: As I have often heard it, I narrate the tale of thy excellences O Lord. If it pleases thee, induce thy craving in me.
Ist (**14,15**/I/46)

1st Guru: No one has found thy worth... Everyone narrates thy

---

Ibid. p. xlvii.

glory as he has repeatedly heard it.
1st (**53**/I/180)

5th Guru: His state, he himself knows. Others speak of him from mere hearsay.
5th (**894**/6/2911)

Revelation

Revelation in the Holy Granth is to be understood in terms of subjective inspiration. The Gurus insist that God cannot be found without but only within man's mind or inner self, as we see from the following couplets.

1st Guru: Men ruin themselves by their search without, while the thing is in the sacred place of their home. The pious receive it in their lap, whilst the perverse miss it through egoism.
1st (**63**/I/214)

1st Guru: Looking around in four directions, I searched my inner self. There I saw the invisible true Lord, the Creator.
1st (**149**/I/497-8)

3rd Guru: O, my mind, within thee is the treasure. Search thou not the thing without.
3rd (**569**/4/1870)

4th Guru: I wandered from village to village and through all the cities, but through the slaves of the Lord I found God in my very mind.
4th (**983**/6/3221-2)

5th Guru: I have given up the search abroad, the Guru has shown my Lord within my home.
5th (**1002**/6/3282)

9th Guru: As fragrance abides in the flower and reflection in the mirror, so dwells God within thee; search for Him within thy heart, O brother!
9th (**984**/4/2240-1)

2. The Ten Gurus

1st Guru Nanak Dev
(1469 - 1539)

2nd Guru Angad
(1504 - 1552)

3rd Guru Amar Das
(1479 - 1574)

4th Guru Ram Das
(1534 - 1581)

5th Guru Arjan Dev
(1563 - 1606)

6th Guru Hargovind
(1595 - 1644)

7th Guru Hari Rai
(1630 - 1661)

8th Guru Hari Krishan
(1656 - 1664)

9th Guru Tegh Bahadur
(1621 - 1675)

10th Guru Govind Singh
(1666 - 1708)

3. Names and titles used for God in the Granth

God is one, but He may be addressed by many names. There is therefore a great variety of names used for God in the Granth. They include Muslim titles, as well as Hindu deities. They reveal God as both *Nirguna* (formless and without attributes) and *Saguna* (with manifest attributes). In Manmohan Singh's Punjabi translation of the Sri Guru Granth Sahib the names of God have generally been termed *Swami, Wahe-guru* or *Hari*. In his English translation they are sometimes transliterated and at other times are rendered *Lord* or *God* or given a qualitative meaning.

The following list is not exhaustive but shows the variety of terms deriving from Hindu, Muslim and original Sikh usage. The reference in brackets after a name gives one instance of its use in the Granth.

HINDU NAMES FOR GOD IN THE GRANTH

ATAM RAM
3rd (**69/1/236**)
BANBARI *5th*
(**79/1/267**)
BHAGVANTA *5th*
(**97/1/322**)
BASUDEV *5th*
(**897/6/2922**)
DAMODAR *5th*
(**98/1/327**)
DEVA *5th*
(**1084/6/3568**)
GOPAL *5th*
(**81/1/272**)
GOVIND *5th*
(**81/1/272**)
HARI *1st*
(**10/1/35**)
ISAR *1st*
(**937/6/3059**)
JAGJIWAN *3rd*
(**126/1/417**)
JAGAN NATH *4th*
(**170/2/570**)
JAGDISHAR *4th*
(**170/2/570**)
JAGDISH
I (**225/2/743**)
KRISHAN MURARE
5th (**98/1/327**)
MURARI
3rd (**30/1/101**)
MADHO *5th*
(**248/2/821**)
MOHAN *5th*
(**1006/6/3295**)
NAR-HARE
4th (**95/1/317**)
NARAYANO *5th*
(**137/1/453**)

PRABHU *1st*
(**17/1/55**)
PRATTIPAAL
5th (**45/1/154**)
PAAR BRAHM *5th*
(**70/1/238**)
RAM *5th*
(**107/1/354**)
SRI DHAR *5th*
(**80/1/269**)
SWAMI *5th*
(**109/1/360**)
SHIVA *5th*
(**207/2/686**)
SIRISHTI NATH
4th (**1115/6/3673**)
THAKUR *5th*
(**99/1/330**)
VISHNU *1st*
(**2/1/4**)
VIDHATA *5th*
(**1086/6/3574**)

SIKH NAMES FOR GOD IN THE GRANTH

AKAAL PURUKH
1st **(1038/6/3409)**
ABINASI PURUKH
4th **(13/1/43)**
EK OANKAR   *1st*
(1/1/1)
GURU   *5th*
(52/1/176)
KARTA PURUKH
1st **(1/1/1)**
KARTAAR
3rd **(89/1/300)**
NIRANJAN   *1st*
(57/1/194)
NIRANKAR   *3rd*
(91/1/306)
PURUKH APAAR
5th **(50/1/169)**
PREETAM   *1st*
(61/1/208)
PURUKH ANANDI
5th **(1096/6/3607)**
SÁT-GURU   *5th*
(825/5/2687)
WAHE-GURU
Has been used in translation

MUSLIM NAMES FOR GOD IN THE GRANTH

ALLAHA   *1*
(64/1/219)
ABDALAH   *5th*
(1083/6/3564)
GUSAIEN   *5th*
(105/1/347)
KARIM   *1st*
(64/1/219)
KHUDA   *5th*
(885/6/2881)
KHASAM   *1st*
(24/1/81)
MAULA   *1st*
(24/1/81)
QADIR   *1st*
(64/1/219)
RAHIM   *1st*
(64/1/219)
SAHIB   *5th*
(70/1/238)

2

THE CONCEPT OF GOD IN THE GRANTH

Introduction

The opening lines of the Granth, known as the *Mool Mantra*, succinctly summarise the definition of God. God is One (*Ek Om*). The Supreme Being is the creator of the universe and its sustainer. He subjects all things to the moral law (*dharma*) and the divine order (*hukam*). God is spoken of both as *Nirguna* (formless and without attributes) and as *Saguna* (manifest with attributes).

As *Nirguna* the Supreme Being is transcendent and unknowable and therefore has to be described in negative terms. This Being is *Agam* (unapproachable), *Agochar* (incomprehensible), *Apaar* (limitless), *Atul* (unweighable), *Alekh* (invisible), *Akah* or *Akath* (indescribable), *Adrisht* (beyond perception) and *Amaap* (immeasurable).

As *Saguna* God is immanent in the world in every thing and every person. He is manifest but not as a creature, for he is never born and never dies, and he has no wife or mother, father or children. He has created himself. The creator is *Nirver* (without rancour or enmity). His divine manifestation is called *Nam* (the name). His names come from both Hindu and Muslim traditions, such as *Pattit-Pavan* (purifier of the fallen), *Rahim* (merciful) and *Karim* (gracious). He is also the destroyer of the wicked (*Nar-Hare*), the purger of pain and the remover of fear.

1. Definitions of God

Mool Mantra

This definition of God is the fundamental or basic creed of the Sikh people. The Granth begins with this creed of Guru Nanak, known as the *Mool Mantra*. The phrase *"Ek Oankar Sat Gur Parsad"* - "there is but one God; by the true Guru's grace he is obtained" - is repeated at the beginning of every new section in the Granth.

Ek Oankar,	There is but one God.
Satti-Nam,	True is his name.
Karta-Purukh,	Creative his personality
Nirbha,	without fear
Nirver,	without enmity
Akaal Murti,	immortal his form
Ajuni,	unborn
Saibhang,	self-illumined
Gur-Parsad,	by Guru's grace (he is obtained).
Adi Sach,	true in the prime
Jugadi Sach,	true in the beginning of ages
Hai Bhi Sach,	true he is even now
Nanak Hosi Bhi Sach.	and true he verily shall be, O Nanak!

1st (**1/1/1**)

Guru Nanak (other definitions)

Unknowable, infinite, unapproachable and imperceptible is my Lord. He is not subject to death and destiny. His caste is castelessness. He is unborn, self-illumined, and without desire or doubt. He has no form, no colour and no features. Through the true name, he becomes manifest.
Ist (**597/4/1961-2**)

He has no mother, father, son or kinsmen. He feels no lust and has no wife. Thou, O Lord, art without ancestry, uncontaminated, endless and infinite. Thy light pervades all. Within every heart is hid the Lord. In all hearts and bodies is his light.
Ist (**597/4/1962**)

Guru Arjan

The Lord himself upholds the universe and shows his omnipotence. He has no hue, form, mouth or beard.
5th (**1346/8/4575**)

My Lord, thou art formless, shapeless, undeceivable, perfect and imperishable. Ever in bliss, ever in bloom, illimitable, beauteous and immaculate.
*5th (***1386/8/4576**)

Wondrous and unequalled is the description of the beauty of the

supreme soul and glorious God.
He is neither old, nor young.
He has no sorrow, nor is he caught in death's noose. He neither perishes nor departs.
In the beginning and commencement of ages, he is contained in the universe.
He feels neither heat, nor cold.
He has no enemy, and he has no friends.
He feels neither joy, nor sorrow.
Everything belongs to him and he is able to do everything.
He has neither father, nor mother.
By vice and virtue, he is unaffected.
Within all hearts, he is always awake.
He is undeceivable, impenetrable, inscrutable and merciful.
5th (**868**/5/2828-9)

2. The Unity of God

*The unity of God is greatly stressed throughout the Granth Sahib. There is but one supreme Lord. There is no second. He is everywhere. He was, he is, and he will be. He is unborn, self-illumined and self-existent. God has two aspects: **saguna**, having related attributes and qualities, and **nirguna**, being unrelated and unknowable as the all-pervading creator.*

There is but one supreme Lord and Master. There is no other.
5th (**45**/1/153)

Nanak, the one Lord is present everywhere. There is no other whatsoever.
1st (**57**/1/193)

The Guru did say, 'God is one and through all the times he is but one and there shall not be any other'.
5th (**99**/I/331)

Besides thee, there is no second. The entire universe is the arena of thy play.
5th (**103**/1/343)

The inaccessible, inapprehensible and unborn Lord is without a Master.
3rd (**118**/1/389)

The true one is ever permanent, he comes and goes not.
3rd (**120-1**/1/399)

Thou art such a merciful and compassionate Lord, that besides thee there is not any other.
3rd (**130**/I/429)

The one Lord pervades all. There is not another.
Ist (**1111**/7/3658-9)

Everyone says and utters, he the Lord is but one.
3rd (**1176**/7/3876)

3. The two aspects of God: Nirguna and Saguna

According to Sikh interpretations the three qualities and the fourth state are two aspects of the same God. The three qualities or modes, in which the world moves, are God's related attributes called Saguna. The fourth state is that in which God existed before creation as the unknowable Nirguna.

He himself is the absolute Lord and verily he is the related one, who by manifesting his power has fascinated the entire world.
5th (**287**/2/958)

From (being) formless, the Lord assumed the immaculate form and from (being) attributeless, he becomes the attributes.
Ist (**940**/6/3073)

The world moves in the three modes, whilst thou, O Lord, abidest in the home of the fourth state.
Ist (**1038**/6/3409)

The creator is the absolute Lord and the creator is the related one.
5th (**862**/5/2806)

The creator is the unmanifest and manifest too is the creator.
5th (**862**/5/2806)

A. God as Transcendent

1. God as Creator

2. God as all pervading, *Nirankar*, or the Formless One

3. God as *Agam, Agochar* and *Apaar*

4. God as Unknowable

5. God as Eternal

Introduction

The transcendent God is so great that he can best be described in negative terms. He is Nirankar *(formless). He is* Agam *(unapproachable)* Agochar *(incomprehensible) and* Apaar *(immeasurable). He is unweighable, immortal, unshakable, unknowable and unlimited. He is imperishable, incalculable, infinite and unfathomable, the highest of the high. The merits of the cosmic Lord cannot be known. He has even created* Brahma, Vishnu *and* Mahesh *for the creation, sustenance and destruction of the universe.*

1. God as Creator

Creator of the World

For countless ages, there was utter darkness. There was no earth and no sky but the infinite Lord's will alone was all pervasive.
There was neither day nor night neither moon nor sun but the Lord alone sat in trance ... There were neither continents nor underworld nor even ocean ... neither was there hell or heaven, or death or time ... There was no Brahma, Vishnu or Shiva ... There was no gopi or Krishna.
Ist (1035/6/3396-7)

When he so willed, then created he the world and without support he sustained the firmament. He created Brahma, Vishnu and Shiva and extended the love of Mammon.
*I*st (**1036**/6/3398-9)

God created the whole world with ease. In the three worlds he is the one luminous Lord.
*I*st (**930**/6/3031)

Creating the creation, thou beholdest it.
*I*st (**934**/6/3049)

This creation, the creator has created.
5th (**885**/6/2883)

Creator of Both Good and Evil

Of the five elements, the Lord created the body and infused into it worldly attachment, falsehood, and self-conceit.
*I*st (**786**/5/2561)

O creator, such a writ hast thou written, thou hast created woe alongside weal.
3rd (**787**/5/2564)

Poison and nectar, the creator has created. To the world-plant, he has attached two fruits.
3rd (**1172**/7/3861)

He himself has created the three qualities and increased love of worldly valuables.
Ist (**1237-8**/7/4079)

Description of the Creator God as Given by the 5th Guru

There is but one God. By the true Guru's grace, he is obtained.
The Lord is the creator of all and he himself enjoys all.
It is the creator who listens and the creator who sees.
The creator is unmanifest and manifest too is the creator.
It is the creator who creates and the creator who destroys.
The creator pervades all and yet detached from all is the creator.
He the maker is the speaker and also the discerner.
It is the maker who comes and goes to the maker.
The creator is the absolute Lord and also the related one.
By the Guru's grace, O Nanak, one and the same view is obtained.
5th (**862**/5/2806)

Description of the Supreme Soul by the 5th Guru

Wondrous and unequalled is the description of the beauty of the supreme soul and glorious God.
He is neither old nor young.
He has no sorrow, nor is he caught in death's noose.

He neither perishes, nor departs.
In the beginning and commencement of the ages, he is contained in the universe.
He feels neither heat nor cold.
He has no enemy, nor friend.
He feels neither joy nor sorrow.
Everything belongs to him and he is able to do everything.
He has neither father nor mother.
He is yonder of the yond and has ever been so.
By vice and virtue, he is not affected.
Within all hearts he is ever awake.
He created the three qualities and maya.
The great maya is his shadow.
5th (**868/5/2828**)

2. God as all pervading, *Nirankar*, or the Formless One

With thy heart behold in every heart the Lord of the world-forest; who fully pervades the ocean and the land.
5th(**79/1/267**)

Of all the hearts, the Lord himself is the enjoyer. The unseen, unapproachable and unlimited Lord pervades everything.
3rd (**113/I/373**)

The reverend true God, the highest of the high.
3rd (**123/I/406**)

Thou art ever safe and sound, O formless one!
1st (**3-4/I/10**)

In the realm of truth (*Sach Khand*) abides the formless Lord.
1st (**8/I/26**)

The true formless Lord is in his own place.
Ist (**14-15/I/46**)

I have found none as great as thee. Thou art contained in the earth, the firmament and the underworlds. Thou dost permeate all places and inter-places. Nanak thou art the true support of thy devotees.
Ist (**74/I/251**)

With thy sight behold in every heart the Lord of the world forest, who entirely pervades the ocean and the land.
5th (**79**/I/267)

Seven islands, seven oceans, nine continents, four Vedas and eighteen Puranas, thou, O Lord, art contained among all and all love thee ... Thou thyself pervadest everything. Thou performest wondrous plays.
3rd (**84**/I/282)

Whithersoever I look, I find my Lord there. Thou, O Lord, the searcher of hearts art contained in all hearts.
4th (**96**/I/321)

The unseen and inscrutable Lord is present everywhere. By no effort can he be obtained. If God shows mercy then is the true Guru met and by his grace man is united with the Lord.
3rd (**127**/I/421)

Within spaces and between spaces thou art. Thou alone, O unique Lord, art all pervading everywhere.
3rd (**131-2**/I/436)

In all hearts the unique Lord is contained. He completely fills the sea, the earth and the sky.
3rd (**133**/I/439)

In every heart the sovereign pervading Lord is contained.
4th (**172**/2/574)

The Lord himself is contained in water and land, O my master. He is all-pervading and is not far off.
4th (**174**/2/582)

The one Lord is without form and yet with form. He is without qualities and yet is with qualities ... Though absolute, he appears to be related.
5th (**250**/2/828)

The Lord has no form or outline or any colour. He is exempt from the three qualities.
5th (**283**/2/943)

Infinite and highest of the high is my master, who is not affected by virtue and vice.
5th (**521**/3/1720)

He has neither form nor outline, neither lineage nor caste; he the perfect Lord completely pervades day and night.
5th (**1086**/6/3572)

Thy slaves live by contemplating and remembering thee, O God, thou dost pervade the woods, the waters and the dry land.
5th (**1085**/6/3569)

Thou art wise, omniscient and beautiful and art contained amongst all.
5th (**1095**/6/3606)

Thou art infinite and joyful, O Lord, and thy light is present everywhere. O, my creator, most revered by men amongst all the

gods, thou art the most luminous Lord. Thou art the imperishable transcendent Lord. How can any tongue utter thy praise?
5th (**1096**/6/3607)

Says Nanak, the Guru has rid me of my doubt. The Muslim God and the Hindus' transcendent Lord are one and the same thing.
5th (**897**/6/2922)

He the formless Lord is himself all in all.
5th (**1001**/6/3279)

The merciful master is fearless and formless.
5th (**1004**/6/3289)

The formless Lord is undeceivable and motionless.
5th (**1083**/6/3561-2)

O my mind, night and day meditate thou on thy formless and self-sustained Lord.
4th (**1201**/7/3960)

The Lord is the highest of the high, immaculate and detached.
5th (**1236**/7/4074)

The formless Lord is contained in his creation.
*I*st (**1107**/7/3645)

Thou fillest ocean, land and sky. Thou, O master, art the overlord of all. Thou, O Lord, art but one Lord, pervading all places and inter-spaces.
4th (**1115**/7/3674)

Says Nanak, the formless supreme Lord is the saviour of his saints.
5th (**1205**/7/3973)

Come ye saints, let us meditate on the eternal Lord, the giver of vital breath and bliss. God, the master of the masterless and the destroyer of the sorrow of the poor permeates all and abides in every heart.
5th (**1206**/7 3974)

The Lord, detached from all, fills all hearts. Thou, O Lord, pervadest every land. Thou hast fashioned the world and created creation from within thee like the waves of the ocean.
5th (**1239**/7/4075)

In all bodies, places, inter-places and countries, the peace-giving, perfect Lord pervades all.
5th (**1237**/7/4076)

O my soul, meditate thou on thy Lord and master, who has no form or sign and is the greatest of the great.
4th (**1297**/8/4280)

By the Guru's instruction, I contemplate my unfathomable God. He, the Lord, has no form or sign.
4th (**1316-17**/8/4345)

Here and there in ten directions the Lord is all pervasive. He is equally contained in the mountains and the stars. Wherever I look, I see the supreme Lord God, my spouse.
5th (**1322**/8/4362)

O, my soul, utter thou the name of the all-pervading Lord.
4th (**1336**/8/4409)

3. God as *Agam*, *Agochar* and *Apaar*

By means of the perfect word, praise thou the Lord, who has no limit or end.
3rd (**68**/I/233)

The transcendent Lord is illimitable, bright, inaccessible, inapprehensible, invisible and inscrutable.
5th (**98**/1/327)

Thou art unapproachable, beyond comprehension, infinite and unfathomable.
5th (**98**/1/328)

Thou art destroyer of pain, priceless treasure, fearless, uninimical, unfathomable, immeasurable, of immortal form, unborn and self-illumined. By pondering over thee, within my mind, I become peaceful.
5th (**99**/I/330)

Unapproachable and beyond comprehension is my Lord. He dwells in every heart and lives nearby.
5th (**106**/I/353)

My Lord is immaculate, inaccessible and infinite. Without a balance, he weighs the world.
3rd (**110**/I/365)

The inaccessible, inapprehensible and unborn Lord is without a master. Through the love of the true Guru, he is obtained.
3rd (**118/1/389**)

Thou alone art unshakeable, unknowable and unlimited. By the Guru's teaching thy knowledge is imparted.
3rd (**120/1/398**)

The lofty unapproachable and immeasurable Lord is the destroyer of ignorance and the dispeller of darkness.
5th (**37/1/454**)

O, my inaccessible and incomprehensible Lord, the life of the world, thou art my mainstay.
5th (**218/2/720**)

The supreme Lord is unapproachable and unfathomable, whosoever utters his name is emancipated.
5th (**271/2/899**)

Through no speech can mortal man reach the master. The Lord is inaccessible, incomprehensible and immaculate.
5th (**287/2/956**)

Nanak, the Lord is unapproachable and illimitable.
5th (**291/2/969**)

Thou art the omnipotent and inaccessible creator, with whom should I compare thee?
4th (**301/2/1006**)

By the Guru's instruction some rare person may meet the infinite unapproachable and incomprehensible Lord.
3rd (**361/3/1204**)

Imperishable, incalculable and unfathomable is the Lord. Within and without, all over, is he.
5th (**456/3/1502**)

The Lord is unapproachable, infinite and unfathomable wisdom, I cannot ascertain his inestimable worth.
5th (**401/3/1330**)

My great Lord is unapproachable, incomprehensible, primal, immaculate, and formless.
4th (**448/3/1476**)

The universe's preserver is incomprehensible, infinite and illimitable. He himself knows his own self.
4th (**448/3/1476**)

Brahma and others like Brahma and the four Vedas proclaim day and night that the Lord is inaccessible, infinite, immaculate, omnipotent, unapproachable and unfathomable.
5th (**535/3/1762**)

Incomparable, illimitable, incomprehensible and immaculate is the Lord who has lured away the whole world.
9th (**537/4/1768**)

Infinite, endless, inaccessible and inapprehensible is the Lord.
*I*st (**634**/4/2082)

Sing thou the praise and glory of the unapproachable and unfathomable Lord.
4th (**699**/4/2285)

My Lord is lofty, unapproachable and infinite. He is ineffable and cannot be described.
5th (**704**/4/2301)

Nanak, my master, is the immeasurable, unfathomable and immovable Lord.
5th (**884**/6/2877)

O, my inaccessible and inapprehensible Lord, thy limit cannot be known.
3rd (**918**/6/2993)

Thou art illimitable, inaccessible and unapproachable, O God! Thou art very high, great and infinite.
5th (**987**/6/3234)

Infinite is the name of the invisible and incomprehensible Lord.
*I*st (**1042**/6/3420)

He is inaccessible and incomprehensible and one cannot evaluate him. Carefree and unfathomable is he in himself.
3rd (**1053**/6/3460-1)

The pious person sings the praise of the name of the Lord, who is

the inaccessible and incomprehensible absolute Lord.
3rd (**1054**/6/3466)

The inaccessible, inapprehensible, carefree and unfathomable Lord is the lover of saints.
3rd (**1055**/6/3469)

O, unfathomable, unknowable, invisible and infinite Lord, no one knows thy bounds.
3rd (**1060**/56/3486-7)

He who knows thy order, praises thy order, O inaccessible, incomprehensible and carefree Lord.
3rd (**1061**/6/3487)

The worth of the unapproachable and incomprehensible Lord cannot be appraised. By the Guru's grace he abides in the mind.
3rd (**1061**/6/3489)

The beneficent venerable Lord is inaccessible and unfathomable.
3rd (**1062**/6/3493)

Unapproachable, inapprehensible and independent is my master. He himself is merciful, boundless and unfathomable.
3rd (**1067**/6/3508)

The unapproachable and inapprehensible Lord is ever imperishable.
4th (**1070**/6/3519)

The Lord is boundless and imperceptible.
5th(**1076/6/3539**)

Thou art unapproachable, compassionate and infinite, O Lord, who can appraise thy worth?
5th (**1094/6/3603**)

The inaccessible and incomprehensible Lord God alone is eternal.
5th (**1101/6/3625**)

My Lord and master is unapproachable, unfathomable, illimitable and the remotest of the remote.
4th (**1114/7/3670**)

Thou, O Lord, art unfathomable, inaccessible and the highest of the high.
5th (**1182/7/3895**)

4. God the Unknowable

O my master, who can know thy merits?
Ist (**156/2/522**)

Thou art ineffable, how canst thou be described?
3rd (**160/2/535**)

The knowledge of the inaccessible and illimitable God is beyond comprehension.
5th (**202/2/672**)

If the unseen Lord can be seen, only then can he be described. Without seeing him, vain is the description.
Ist (**222/2/734**)

Thy condition and estimation thou thyself knowest. None else, O Nanak, knows thy praise.
5th (**266/2/884**)

Nanak of that Lord, no one has found the limits. All the demigods are tired of searching.
5th (**284/2/945**)

I am astonished at the wonderful mystery of the Lord. Nanak, thy condition, thou thyself knowest, O Lord!
5th (**291/2/971**)

He alone knows what is in his mind.
5th (**294/2/982**)

The merits of the cosmic Lord cannot be known, Nanak, he is all wonder.
5th (**299**/2/997)

Of what type or sort is that gate and of what type or sort is the mansion wherein residing, thou takest care of all, O Lord? My master, thy limit cannot be known. The indescribable God cannot be described.
3rd (**835**/3/1436)

The universe preserver is incomprehensible, infinite and illimitable. He himself knows his own self. What should these poor creatures utter, which may amount to narrating and describing thee, O Lord?
4th (**448**/3/1476)

Shiva, Brahma and all the silent sages cannot gauge or seize the Lord's condition.
5th (**498**/3/1642)

No one knows God's state. The renunciators, celibates, penitents and a good many wise men have utterly failed.
9th (**537**/4/1768)

Unfathomable, is thy knowledge, O infinite creator. I am low and know nothing.
5th (**547**/4/1799)

Thou appearest not unto me, though thou abidest with all. How can the thirst in me, the thirsty one abate, when there is a screen between the lake and me?
Ist (**557**/4/1832)

Says Nanak, what shall I give him, who gives me a message from that master of mine? Cutting off my head, I will give it to him to sit on and without a head, I will perform his service.
Ist (**558**/4/1835)

Wherever I look, there I find thy light. Of what sort is thy form?
Ist (**596**/4/1960)

I know not how to meditate on God. I only repeat God, God, Guru, Guru ...
The Lord is limitless. I can only describe him within limits. What do I know, what is he like?
5th (**612**/4/2010)

Everywhere the supreme Lord completely pervades all. Where does he go and where does he come from?
5th (**615**/4/2020)

O my mother, in what way can I see the Lord of the world? In the darkness of great worldly love and spiritual ignorance my mind remains entangled.
9th (**632**/4/2075)

The Lord God is beyond reach; say how can one attain to him? He has neither form nor sign and is unseen. Tell me then, O saints, how is he to be remembered?
3rd (**644**/4/2112-3)

He is the formless, immaculate and unapproachable Lord. What excellences of his should one narrate and sing?
3rd (**644**/4/2113)

Thy colour is known not, nor is thy form seen. Who can realise thy power?
5th (**670**/4/2197)

Thou art the true creator and the unknowable maker.
1st (**688**/4/2253)

The pure Lord abides within my mind, but I know not his secret.
9th (**703**/4/2298)

Says Nanak, hear my supplication, O happy bride, and tell me what my beloved looks like?
5th (**703**/4/2300)

Shiva and thirty-three million gods contemplate the Lord, but know not his secret.
4th (**719**/4/2349)

O my venerable beloved, I know not thy limits.
1st (**730**/5/2383)

What is the scale and what the weights? What assayer shall I call for thee, O Lord?
1st (**730**/5/2383

What am I poor mortal? I cannot describe even a hair of thine. My infinite Lord, Brahma, Shiva,
adepts, silent sages and Indra know not thy state.
5th (**822**/5/2677)

I know not thy end, O my Lord. What wisdom can a blind man have like me?
1st (**795**/5/2590)

How can the immeasurable Lord be measured? If anyone else be as great as he, then only can he understand him. Without him there is not another. How can his worth be ascertained?
3rd (**797**/5/2595)

God's mystery, the Vedas know not.
5th (**837**/5/2726)

The yogis, the celibates, the vegetarians and the hermits cannot find the limits of the imperishable Lord. Shiva and the gods bewail and bemoan, but they know not even one iota of the invisible and inscrutable Lord.
5th (**867**/5/2824)

The creator alone knows its worth. What can the poor creature know?
5th (**883**/6/2876)

The Vedas know not God's greatness. Brahmins cannot realise his secrets. The incarnations know not his bounds. Infinite is God, the transcendent Lord.
5th (**894**/6/2911)

His state, he himself knows. Others speak of him from mere hearsay ... Shiva knows not the Lord's way. The gods have grown weary searching for him. The goddesses know not his mystery.
5th (**894**/6/2911-12)

He who created continents, spheres and the universe, that Lord cannot be known.
1st (**907**/6/2957)

The Lord himself creates his own self. The unseen Lord cannot be seen.
3rd (**912**/6/2972)

No one has found thy end. Thou alone knowest thy self.
3rd (**918**/6/2993)

What can man say of the Lord, he whom man cannot see.
1st (**937**/6/3061)

Millions have made efforts, but have not found the limits of the Lord.
4th (**984**/6/3224)

Luminous and infinite is my Lord. Who can know thy wonderful play? The limits of thy yonder shore one cannot fathom.
5th (**988**/6/3237)

Countless beings utter the Lord's merits. How can I narrate them? Even the greatest of the great know not the limits of the Lord.
1st (**1033**/6/3388)

If thou revealest not thyself, no one can understand thee.
1st (**1034**/6/3393)

His limits no one knows. It is through the perfect Guru that I have obtained understanding.
1st (**1039**/6/3399)

Brahma, Vishnu and Shiva serve the Lord. They cannot know the extent of the invisible and inscrutable Lord.
3rd (**1053**/6/3462)

O unfathomable, unknowable, invisible and infinite Lord, no one knows thy bounds.
3rd (**1060**/6/3486-7)

Which of thy virtues can my tongue utter? The thousand-headed serpent knows not thy limits. Day and night he utters thy new name, but he cannot describe even one of thy virtues, O Lord.
5th (**1083**/6/3562)

Thy form cannot be known. How can one meditate on thee?
5th (**1095**/6/3604)

He is invisible and cannot be seen. How can I describe him?
1st (**1170**/7/3853)

What can I, a worm-like creature, say? No one has found thy beginning or end, O my Lord!
3rd (**1172**/7/3861)

He is illimitable, who can find his limit?
5th (**1188**/7/3917)

I ask the saints as to what my Lord is like? I surrender my soul to him, who gives me news of him. Give thou me news of him and tell me what my master is like and where the bewitcher resides?
5th (**1237**/7/4076)

People reflect on nine grammars, six *Shashtras* and the six chapters of the Vedas and night and day utter the *Mahabharaat* in eighteen divisions. Even then they cannot find thy limits, O Lord! ... Abiding in the navel, Brahma knows not the Lord's end.
Ist (**1237**/7/4078)

Of himself, the Lord created himself and he alone knows himself.
Ist (**1279**/7/4218)

Lotus-like thou sittest in trance and art hid from the eyes. Brahma is called great, but he too knows not thy limit. He has no father or mother; who has begotten thee, O my Lord.
Ist (**1279**/7/4219)

It is the Lord who created Brahma, Vishnu, Shiva and other gods. He blessed Brahma with the Vedas and yoked him to adoration of the Lord. The Lord created ten incarnations, of whom one was king Rama.
2nd (**1279**/7/4220)

The nine great yogis, six celibates, eighty-four men of miracles and religious guides - of these none knows the limits of the Lord.
3rd (**1282**/7/4229)

O great God, thou art supremely unfathomable and unknowable. Searching for thee, I am tired but I have found not thy limits.
4th (**1296**/8/4277)

O Lord, on what sort of seat art thou seated, whereon thou givest thought to thy creatures?
5th (**1305**/8/4308)

O treasure of virtues, I know not thy limits.
Ist (**1342-3**/8/4430)

5. God as Eternal

I have contracted love with that true Lord! He dies not, nor comes and goes.
5th (**46**/1/157)

The Lord dies not, nor is there any mourning for him.
Ist (**9-10**/I/32)

Call him permanent, whose Lord hears not the writ of destiny. The sky and earth shall pass away. Ever stable is he alone.
Ist (**64**/1/219)

I have obtained the God of immortal form as my spouse. He is imperishable and so dies and goes not.
4th (**78**/1/265)

The almighty God never dies or goes. What he gives, ever continues increasing.
4th (**79**/1/266)

Thou art the unborn, self-illumined and immortal being.
5th (**916**/6/2985)

The world is the reflection of him, who has no father and mother. He has earned neither sister nor brother. He is without birth and death, lineage and caste. He, who ages not, is pleasing to my mind.
Ist (**1038**/6/3408)

Thou art the immortal Lord, over thy head there is no death.
Ist (**1038**/6/3409)

His is the fruitful sight and immortal form, which perishes never, unborn and self-illumined.
5th (**1082**/6/3560)

O, my imperishable, eternal and inapprehensible Lord, everything is attached to thee.
5th (**1082**/6/3560)

My master is the imperishable, transcendent Lord.
5th (**1082**/6/3559)

The Lord is known to be imperishable, unborn and ever stable, primordial is his true mansion.
Ist (**1112**/7/3659)

Man, led astray by doubt, does false things. Without birth and death is the omnipresent Lord. After preparing sweets, thou stealthily givest them to thy stone god to eat. O, ignorant worshipper of mammon, the Lord is not born, nor does he die. Let that mouth be burnt, which says that the Lord enters into existences. He is not born, nor does he die. He neither comes nor goes.
5th (**1136**/7/3737)

O, my soul, contemplate thou the fearless Lord, who is true, ever true. He is without enmity; the

being beyond time, unborn and self-illumined.
4th (**1201**/7/3960)

The immaculate Lord, who created his own self, is all by himself.
*I*st (**1237**/7/4078)

B. God As Immanent

1. God as Sustainer

2. God as Merciful and Compassionate

3. God as Cause and Doer of Everything

4. God as Everything

5. God as Destroyer

6. God Leads Some and Misleads Others

7. God as Father and Mother

Introduction

The Granth also views God as immanent, the one who is in every heart. His light shines within all souls. The Lord is near. Deem God not afar off, says the Guru. He is all-pervading, the cause and doer of everything, both good and evil. Mortals are simply instruments in the Lord's hands, and they play as he makes them play. He is deemed to be father and mother, who is merciful and compassionate and sustains everything. He is both subject and object. He himself is everything and there is no second. He both leads and misleads. None can guide them whom God himself misleads, as he yokes some to falsehood and deception. He is the destroyer of the wicked. God himself creates and destroys. He is everything and all-pervading.

Amongst all there is light and that light art thou. By his light, the light shines within all souls. By the Guru's teaching the divine light becomes manifest.
Ist (**13**/1/42)

Thou art the river, all-knowing and all-being. How can I, a fish, find thy limits? Wherever I look, there thou art. Getting out of thee, I burst and die.
Ist (**25**/1/85)

O my Lord, wondrous are thy plays. Thou dost completely pervade ocean, earth and sky and art thyself contained amongst all. Wheresoever I look, there I find thy light.
Ist (596/4/1959-60)

The flower-girt Lord is contained in every heart. In ocean, earth and sky, he is unmanifestly contained. By the Guru's instruction he is seen.
Ist (597-8/4/1964)

Showering his benediction on me the great true Guru has shown me the Lord, in the mortal world, the nether world and the firmament.

He, the unborn Lord, is and also shall be. In thy heart see thou him, the enemy of pride.
Ist (598/4/1964)

The Lord is not far off. In all hearts all mortals are his brides.
Ist (765/5/2491)

Within all hearts he is ever awake.
5th (868/5/2828)

He who created creation is ever present. See him not far away.
3rd (909/6/2964)

Let man know the one Lord within and without; by this shall he realise the Lord's presence in his very home. The Lord is near. Deem God not afar off.
Ist (930/6/3033)

1. God as Sustainer

God sustains his creation. He looks over it and cares for it. He cherishes his creation.

The soul and body are all his. Man eats what he gives.
Ist (465/3/1535)

Know the true creator to be true. He is the true sustainer of all ... Creating the two millstones of the earth and the sky, he has separated them ... The Lord created the sun and the moon. He sees that they are ever on the move.
Ist (580/4/1906)

He who created the world watches over it and yokes the mortals to their tasks.
Ist (765/5/2493)

Note: The Holy Granth has scores of references about this subject which can be traced easily from the pages of the Granth.

2. God as Merciful and Compassionate

God is merciful to the poor, cherisher of the world and master of the universe.
5th (**98**/1/327)

O my beloved Lord! Thou art the world cherisher, kind, blissful, deep, profound, infinite, the master of the universe.
5th (**98-9**/1/329/330)

The Lord is kind, merciful and compassionate; all are satiated and satisfied through him.
5th (**103**/1/343)

My Lord is the highest of the high. Showing his mercy, he blends the person with himself.
3rd (**112**/1/370)

Thou art merciful and ever the peace giver.
3rd (**122**/1/405)

Thou art such a merciful and compassionate Lord that besides thee there is no other.
3rd (**130**/1/429)

The merciful luminous Lord is the master of the poor and the saviour of sinners.
5th (**137**/1/453)

The merciful master is fearless and formless.
5th (**1005**/6/3293)

He is pleased with devotional service and he the merciful master of the meek is softened not through any other merit.
5th (**1083**/6/3561-2)

3. God as Cause and Doer of Everything

This will raise some moral questions as to the moral freedom enjoyed by man. If all actions both good and bad are done and controlled by God, then where lies the responsibility of man in becoming a sinner? It places man in the position of a puppet and all responsibility lies with the puppeteer (God) for every wrong doing. Man does not seem to enjoy free moral choice, hence he cannot be punished for his actions, which are controlled by God himself. It makes God himself the author, sustainer and promoter of evil in this world. How can a moral God punish people for sins, which they have not committed with free moral choice?

Pious persons obtain the name and the self-willed lose it. Thou thyself separatest mortals and thyself unitest them.
*I*st (**11**/1/37)

He himself does and causes others to do. Everything is in his hands. He himself slays and revives. Within and without, he is with the mortal.
5th (**48**/1/161)

Of himself he does and of himself he causes others to do. Some he blesses by raising them from slumber. By merging man in his name, God himself unites him in union with him.
3rd (**69**/I/235)

God himself causes mortals to do evil deeds and good ones. Nothing lies in the power of human being.
4th (**77**/I/261)

In thy will man wanders in the wilderness and in thy will he finds the right path.
5th (**98**/1/328)

Thou thyself makest men do various deeds night and day and thou unitest them with the congregation of the saints.
3rd (**113**/1/375)

The Lord does everything, with whom can anyone lodge a complaint? The mortal may grumble if he were to err. Nanak, the Lord acts and causes everything to be done.
3rd (**114**/I/377)

The creator himself makes us work. What can someone else do? What can be done by his doing?
3rd (**124**/1/410)

The creator himself does and causes others to do. He himself enshrines the Guru's hymns in man's mind.
3rd (**125**/1/415)

The Lord acts and causes others to act. He himself establishes and disestablishes. Without thee, O

Lord, nothing can be done. Thou thyself hast engaged mortals in various tasks. He causes death and he revives. Uniting with the guild of saints, he blends mortals with his own self.
3rd (**125-6/I/416**)

What the creator does that comes to pass. By man's effacing effort it cannot be effaced.
Ist (**139/1/462**)

God himself is the Lord, both an attendant and a devotee. God himself acts and causes others to act.
3rd (**550/4/1809**)

God himself beholds and also rejoices. As he wills so does he yoke mortals to their tasks. Some the Lord himself puts on the right path and some the Lord leads astray into the wilderness.
3rd (**550/4/1810**)

The Lord himself is the field and the farmer and he grows and grinds the corn. He cooks and he gives dishes and puts food on them. He himself sits down to eat it.
3rd (**550/4/1811**)

The creator grants weal and woe and he gives gifts.
3rd (**551/5/1813**)

Nanak, the Lord himself does everything and he himself makes others act.
3rd (**769/5/2506**)

As thou movest and as it pleases thee, O illustrious Lord, so does anyone move.
3rd (**797/5/2597**)

The Lord himself makes men do the deeds and takes no blame on himself.
5th (**803**/5/2617)

Nanak, mortals are instruments in the Lord's hands. So they play as he makes them play. As he wills so that road they tread.
4th (**834/5/2716**)

Some are the Lord's slaves and some are gone astray in doubt. God himself acts and causes everything to be done.
3rd (**842/5/2745**)

With whatever thou yokest anyone, to that he is yoked. None is foolish, nor is anyone wise.
5th (**914/6/2980**)

God himself infuses pain and pleasure within mortal man and leads him into doubt. The Lord causes some to miss his name and to some he reveals it through the Guru.
3rd (**912/6/2973**)

God himself yokes mortals to virtue and vice. They do only what the creator himself makes them do.
3rd (**950/6/3111**)

To whatever the Lord yokes them, to that they remain yoked. What can those poor creatures do?
3rd (**951**/6/3115)

Some he has yoked to falsehood and deception; such apostates are ruined.
3rd (**952**/6/3115)

Who can show the path to him, whom I lead astray from the very outset?
*I*st (**952**/6/3119)

He, whom the Lord has blinded, the Lord alone can cause to see clearly.
2nd (**954**/6/3127)

Whither thou attachest the mortal, O Lord, thither he is attached. Why should he blame anyone, when thou so willest?
5th (**960**/6/3147)

By himself man is neither ignorant nor wise. As the Lord makes man do, so is he known.
5th (**1004**/6/3289)

As thou drivest me, so am I driven, and within my mouth I enshrine thy ambrosial name.
*I*st (**1012**/6/3316)

As thou willest so dost thou make men walk. Everyone acts according to the order issued by thee.
*I*st (**1031**/6/3381)

Both union and separation my Lord has created. Creating the creation, he has endowed it with weal and woe.
*I*st (**1032**/6/3386)

God alone is the giver of merit and demerit. Rare is the person who understands this by the Guru's grace.
3rd (**1052**/6/3459)

The creator Lord himself acts and causes everything to be done. As he wills, so drives he mortals.
3rd (**1061**/6/3488)

The creator Lord himself acts and makes others act, and he himself leads one astray to doubt. Of himself the Lord causes everything to be done and of himself he yokes each to his task.
3rd (**1061**/6/3489)

My creator Lord, thou thyself art the doer of deeds.
5th (**1076**/6/3540)

He himself leads some astray in doubt and fruitless are their deeds.
*I*st (**1090**/6/3589)

As the Lord himself makes man dance, so dances he, O Nanak!
3rd (**1094**/6/3601)

As thou thyself makest them walk, so do they walk; nothing lies in the power of the creatures.
5th (**1095**/6/3606)

4. God as Everything

As creator God is both subject and object. He himself is everything. He himself is fish and he is water. He himself is the Vedas, the Puranas and all the Shashtras and he utters them all. He himself is the ocean, the ship and the one who ferries it across the terrible seas. He himself is the Yogi, performing penance. He is the Guru and the disciple, and he himself imparts instruction. He creates and destroys. He is air, water, fire, sun, moon, male and female, flower and the bumble bee, fish, tortoise and cause of all causes. He is the deity, the temple and the worshipper.

This makes God everything and there is no other. Man is reduced to being a plaything, a tool in God's hands, who cannot be held responsible for his deeds, as it is God himself who performs all actions. If God is everything, then God himself must take the responsibility for all evil in this world, and not man who after all is God himself. Man is helpless and dependent on the whim of God for his salvation.

God himself is the master and the servant. How insignificant the man is, O Nanak.
Ist (**10-11**/1/35)

Thou thyself art the giver and the enjoyer. Beside thee, I know of none other.
Ist (**11**/1/35)

The Lord himself is the relisher, he is the relish and the enjoyer. He himself is the vesture (bride) and the couch and bridegroom. He himself is the fisherman and the fish and he is both the water and the net. He himself is the metal ball of the net and the bait within. My maid! My beloved is in everyway playful ... Prays Nanak, listen to my supplication. Thou art the tank and thou art the swan. Thou art the lotus and thou art the water lily. Thou art pleased on beholding (them).
Ist (**23**/1/78)

The Lord himself is everything. There is no other, no second ... Thou, O Lord art thy own excellences and thou thyself utterest, hearest and ponderest over them. Thou thyself art the jewel of the name and its assayer and thou thyself art infinite value.
Ist (**54**/I/184)

Thou thyself art the pure gem and also the colour of madder. Thou thyself art the pure pearl and also the devotee and intercessor.
Ist (**54**/1/184)

Thou thyself art the water and also the fish. By thy own self thou art the net. Thou thyself castest the net and also art the film on the water.
1st (**84-5/I/285**)

God himself is the king and also the subject. He himself is the ascetic and the enjoyer.
5th (**97/I/324**)

Thou art unqualitative, qualitative and the peace giver. Thou art un-affected, the enjoyer and imbued in affection. Thy ingenuities thou thyself knowest. It is thou who rememberest thyself. Thou art the master and thou art the servant. Thou, O Lord art unmanifest and manifest as well.
5th (**102-3/I/341**)

God himself is the maker and the enjoyer ... The unseen who himself causes to be seen.
3rd (**125/I/415**)

The Lord himself is mammon (*maya*) and also its spiritual ig-norance. He himself has infused affection for it in the whole world.
3rd (**125/I/415**)

God himself is devotee and also his master. He is imbued with himself.
5th (**498/3/1642**)

God himself is the banker, the merchant and the shop. He him-self is the ocean, the ship and the ferryman. The Lord is the Guru, the disciple and shows the wharf.
3rd (**517/3/1705**)

The Lord himself is the field, the farmer and he grows and grinds the corn. He cooks and he gives dishes and puts food in them. He himself sits down to eat it.
3rd (**550/4/1811**)

He is the water, and gives the toothpick. He offers water for gargling.
3rd (**551/4/1811**)

The Lord himself is Vedas and Puranas and all the Shashtras. He himself utters them and he is pleased.
3rd (**551/4/1813**)

The creator sits down to worship and creates the world. He, himself is a householder and a renouncer. He utters the unutterable. The creator grants weal and woe and he gives gifts.
3rd (**551/4/1813**)

He is the terrible ocean, the ship, the helmsman and he ferries beings across it.
3rd (**552/4/1815**)

He is the Lord, an attendant and he is the destroyer of sins.
3rd (**552/4/1816**)

The Lord himself is the school, the teacher and brings the pupils to be coached. He himself is the father, the mother and he makes the children wise. In one place,

he himself reads and understands everything, in another place he makes men puerile.
3rd (**552**/4/1818)

The Lord is the good man, heavenly herald and the celestial singer and he is the utterer of the six schools of philosophy. The Lord himself is the God of creation, the God of death and the God of nutrition. Through the Guru, he himself narrates the unnarratable story. He himself is the renunciator, and enjoyer and becoming a solitary he walks about in the wilderness. The Lord discourses with himself; he instructs and is discreet, graceful and wise. Staging his play, he himself beholds it. The Lord himself is the knower of all beings.
3rd (**553**/4/1819)

He created the eighteen castes and the exalted Lord himself rules over his domain. He destroys, he redeems and by his grace he pardons.
3rd (**553**/4/1821)

The creator himself is the sixty-eight holy places and also bathes in them. The Lord practises self-abstinence and makes men repeat his name.
5th (**554**/4/1822)

The Lord himself is the eighteen loads of vegetation and makes it bear fruit. He is the gardener and irrigates all the plants and puts

their fruit in his mouth. He is the maker and the enjoyer. He himself gives and makes others give. He himself is the Lord, the protector and is contained in his creation.
3rd (**554**/4/1823-4)

Nanak, the Lord has separated some from himself and some he has attached to his name.
3rd (**554**/4/1839)

The beloved hears and sees all and utters from the mouth through the mouths of all. My beloved himself leads mortals into the wilderness and shows the way. The beloved creates creation and at his destroying it is destroyed. My beloved is both the wharf and the ferryman and ferries beings across. My beloved is the ocean and the boat and the Guru, the boatman who pilots it.
4th (**604**/4/1986)

The Lord himself is in the egg-born, foetus-born, sweat-born and the earth-born. He himself is in the continents and in all the worlds. He himself is the thread and the many beads. Exercising his might, he has strung the worlds.
4th (**605**/4/1987)

Amongst all hearts, the beloved enjoys himself. He, the Lord is contained within all men and women. The darling himself is all-in-all. He himself establishes and disestablishes. The darling beholds and rejoices. He the Lord

himself works miracles (plays)
and sees them.
4th (**605**/4/1988)

My darling himself is the pilgrim
station and the raft and the Lord
ferries beings across.
4th (**605**/4/1988)

My darling himself is the yogi's
personality and performs penance.
He himself is the true-born Guru
and the disciple. The Lord himself
imparts instruction ... The Lord
praises his own self. Slave Nanak
is satiated with the Lord's elixir.
4th (**505**/4/1989)

The dear Lord obeys his will and
gives the command.
4th (**606**/4/1991)

The beloved is the milkmaid and
Krishna and he himself grazes the
cows in the jungle.
4th (**606**/4/1992)

The omnipotent and omnipresent
creator is himself the doer of
deeds.
5th (**618**/4/2028-9)

The Lord himself grants gifts and
himself receives them.
5th (**710**/4/2323)

The Lord himself is spiritualism
and materialism. He himself instructs and becomes manifest.
The Lord himself is the true Guru
and he is the Guru's words.
Nanak, the Lord himself utters
and preaches the Guru's word.
3rd (**797**/5/2596)

O master, thou thyself art the
Guru, the disciple and the treasure
of virtues.
3rd (**797**/5/2597)

The entire universe is the manifestation of one God. The Lord
himself is the trade and the
trader. The unqualified Lord of
form assumes many forms in the
qualitative state. He himself is
the water and the waves.
*5th (***803**/5/2616)

He himself is the temple and the
worship. He is the worshipper
and the god (*deva*).
5th (**803**/5/2616)

The Lord creates and he supports
... He is mute and the utterer. He
is undeceivable and cannot be deceived. He is unmanifest and
manifest, he pervades all hearts
and remains detached. He, himself is absolute and he is with the
world.
5th (**803**/5/2617)

The Lord is the creator of all and
he himself enjoys all. It is the
creator who listens and the creator
who sees. He, the creator is unmanifest and manifest. It is the
creator who creates and the
creator who destroys. The creator
pervades all and the creator is also
detached from all. He, the maker
is the speaker and the discerner.
It is the maker who comes and
goes to the maker. The creator is
the absolute Lord and the related
one.
5th (**862**/5/2806)

He himself is with form and form-less.
5th (**863**/5/2811)

Thou thyself createst and destroy-est. Thou puttest everyone to task.
Thou thyself art air, water and fire and thyself unitest one in union with thee.
Thou thyself art the moon, the sun and the most perfect of the perfect.
Thou thyself art the male and the female.
Thou thyself art the chessboard and the chess-man.
Thou thyself art the bumble-bee, the flower, the fruit and the tree.
Thou thyself art the water, the desert, the ocean and the tank.
Thou thyself art the big fish, the tortoise and the cause of causes.
Thy form cannot be known.
*I*st (**1020**/6/3344-5)

He himself is the bow and the bowman. He himself is omni-scient, beautiful and wise. He alone is the utterer, orator and hearer. He himself has made the entire lot.
*I*st (**1021**/6/3345)

Thou thyself art the fish and the net. Thou thyself art the cow and the grazier. Thou thyself art with-out speech, without form, without fear and wrapt in trance.
*I*st (**1021**/6/3346)

He himself is the celibate, the man of chastity and contentment, and himself does all deeds.
*I*st (**1021**/6/3347)

In the continents, solar systems, nether regions, spheres and the three worlds, the Lord is sitting in trance.
*I*st (**1023**/6/3353)

God himself speaks and makes man speak. The non-eating Lord, is immaculate and formless.
4th (**1135**/7/3735)

The Lord himself is *Lakhshmi* and the spouse.
Installing the world, he himself enjoys it.
God himself is calf, cow and milk.
He himself is the support of the temple of the body.
He himself is the deed and the doer.
He himself becoming the Guru-word reflects upon himself.
*I*st (**1290**/7/3924)

5. God as Destroyer

Destroyer of the World

He, who builds all, demolishes as well.
1st (934/6/3046)

Breaking and crushing the Lord fashions, and fashioning and making he again shatters.
The demolished ones he builds and the built ones he demolishes.
The omnipotent, carefree Lord dries up the full tanks and again fully fills them.
1st (935/6/3052)

The adorner, by his command demolishes and having demolished himself constructs.
Whatever pleases the all-powerful Lord, that happens.
1st (579/4/1903)

Destroyer of the Wicked

The Lord has smitten the wicked and the evil. His slaves' honour the creator has preserved.
5th (201/2/668)

They who are smitten by the supreme Lord are no one's property. It is real justice that they who bear enmity to the one who is without enmity (God) should perish.
4th (206/2/1023)

Slaying the demons the Lord saves the saints.
1st (224-5/2/742)

He who slanders thy attendants, thou crushest and destroyest.
3rd (517/3/1704)

The Lord instantaneously destroys the slanderers. He allows them not even to stay for a trice.
5th (523/3/1727)

I have heard this old story uttered by the devotees, that the Lord cuts into pieces all the wicked and blesses his slaves with honour.
5th (815/5/2653)

My true Lord is the destroyer of demons.
3rd (1056/6/3470)

The revered God, the Lord of the universe, is the destroyer of devils.
5th (1082/6/3559)

Whosoever shows disrespect to the Lord's slave; him the Lord destroys.
5th (1235/7/4071)

It is the creator who creates and the creator who destroys.
5th (862/5/2806)

6. God Leads Some and Misleads Others

God leads some to understanding and leads others astray in doubt. This is a difficult thing to understand, that God being a moral God, should lead some to the right path and mislead others to destruction. We see this issue has even baffled the Gurus. The third Guru says that the Lord has hoodwinked the world and man has no say in it. Again he says, "What can the poor creatures do, when thou misleadest them?"
The answer to this to some extent, according to the doctrine of Karma, must lie with man's previous deeds and God's writ on the basis of past deeds. Still the issue is not fully resolved.

He whom the Lord himself has put on the wrong track has no caste and no honour.
5th (**42**/1/143)

This world has gone astray in doubt. Thou thyself, O Lord, hast misled it
Ist (**72**/1/244)

By himself, God leads man astray in doubt and himself imparts understanding.
4th (**82**/1/276)

Whose support can he seek, whom the Lord himself misleads? What is pre-prescribed, that cannot be erased.
3rd (**110**/1/365)

World-hardened men, who eat poison by repeatedly telling lies, the Lord himself has led astray.
Ist (**145-6**/1/484)

Thou thyself leadest mortals astray and they forget thy name. O Lord, showering thy benedictions on them, thou savest some.
Ist (**416**/3/1380)

He himself misleads man and puts him on the right path.
Ist (**424**/3/1406)

Proud apostates know not the worth of worshipping the Lord. The Lord himself has beguiled them; they lose their lives as in a gamble.
3rd (**425**/3/1417)

Spiritual ignorance is diffused amongst all. Doubt is thy doing, O Lord.
Having created doubt, thou thyself causest man to stray. Those on whom thy grace rests, the Guru meets.
Ist (**433**/3/1427-8)

The true Lord has himself beguiled thee, O fool. It was so ordained on thy brow.
3rd (**435**/3/1435)

The Lord himself has misled them and put them on the evil track. Nothing lies in their power ... Thus says Nanak, what can the poor creatures do, when thou

misleadest them in doubt?
3rd (**441**/3/1456)

The true Lord has hoodwinked the world. Man has no say in it.
3rd (**492**/3/1623)

When it pleases God, he causes the soul to wander. Then he sets in motion this world play.
3rd (**514**/3/1692)

He whom the master himself leads astray, ever continues coming and going.
5th (**523**/3/1727)

The perverse are led astray from the very beginning. Within them is avarice and ego.
3rd (**549**/4/1804)

An apostate abandons ambrosia and amasses poison. The creator himself has infatuated him.
3rd (**644**/4/2112)

Creating creation, the Lord yokes each one to the task.
Some he engages in his devotional service and some he leads astray.
Some he puts on the right path and some he goads into the wilderness.
3rd (**644**/4/2114)

His affairs are not accomplished. He is fascinated by mammon (*maya*). What can the helpless creature do, when the Lord himself leads him astray?
5th (**707**/4/2314)

Ministering the intoxicating potion, the Lord himself misleads mortals. Nanak, the writ of past deeds cannot be effaced.
5th (**1005**/6/3292)

When duped by the Lord, he automatically goes astray.
3rd (**1048**/6/3443)

The sense of mine and thine, thou thyself hast created.
3rd (**1062**/6/3493)

He alone strays whom the Lord himself leads astray and he alone understands whom he instructs.
5th (**1075**/6/3537)

When thou thyself causest me to stray, to whom should I go to complain?
Ist (**1188**/7/3915)

Ministering the intoxicating herb, the Lord himself has caused men to go astray, and so he is born again and again .
5th (**1223-4**/7/4032)

Ministering to him the potion of sins, the true Lord has caused him to go astray.
5th (**1224**/7/4032)

O, brother, no one knowingly strays from the path. He alone strays, whom God himself misleads and he alone is enlightened, whom he enlightens.
Ist (**1344**/8/4434)

7. God as Father and Mother

The divine mother, formulating a plan of propagation, installed the three deities.
*I*st (**7**/1/22)

The one Lord is brother, the one is the real friend and the one is my mother and father.
5th (**45**/1/152)

Thy child has made mistakes and untoward overtures. Thou O God art my father and mother.
5th (**51**/1/174)

My father! I know not which is thy way?
5th (**51**/1/175)

He is sweeter than mother and father.
5th (**73**/1/248)

He has become merciful to me like mother and father and has cherished me like his own child.
5th (**381**/3/1268)

I am thy child and thou, O Lord, art my father. Forgive thou thy serf Nanak and blend him with thyself.
4th (**881**/6/2868)

I am thy child and thou art my father. Thou puttest milk into my mouth.
5th (**884**/6/2878)

Thou blessest thy saints with the gift of meditating on thee. Nanak too begs for thee, O Lord, my mother.
5th (**916**/6/2985)

Says Nanak, O saints, God alone is my intimate friend, wealth, youth, son, father and mother.
3rd (**917**/6/2991)

God himself is the mother and himself the father, who creating man has shown him the world.
3rd (**921**/6/3003)

Like mother and father, the Lord hugs me to his bosom and cherishes me like his tiny child.
5th (**957**/6/3138)

3

THE NATURE OF THE WORLD

Introduction

The concept of the world in the Granth is no different from what is commonly found in Hinduism. The world is created and destroyed at will by God, who watches over it from a trance-like state. It is illusion (*maya*) and a plaything (*lila*) of God. Therefore it is not real but only a passing phase. The Supreme Lord has created Brahma, Vishnu and Mahesh with three functions, to create, sustain and destroy the cosmos continually. God lures the world away from himself through *maya* (translated by Manmohan Singh as "mammon"). As for man, he is attached to this world by the three qualities (*gunas*) of matter: *rajas* (passion), *tamas* (darkness) and *sattva* (goodness), which increase his love for earthly values.

As the primal being, God is the support and upholder of the earth. God's *dharma* sustains creation through its moral law. The supreme being is not only the creator of this world but of many more worlds beyond. There is an imaginary bull that supports the weight of this earth, according to this quote from Guru Nanak:

How much load is there on the bull? If someone understands this, he becomes the true man. There are more worlds beyond this earth, more and more.
1st (3/1/9)

1. An Account of Creation based on Lunar Days

The first lunar day, the unique Lord is peerless, immortal, unborn, without caste and involvement. He is unapproachable and inapprehensible and has no form or outline.

The second lunar day, they who are yoked to love of another, regret it in the end. They are bound at *yama's* (death's) door and continue coming and going.
Creating the spheres the Lord has established them apart and shall ultimately destroy them.
The earth and the sky he has made places for habitation. He has created the night and day, fear and love.

The third lunar day the Lord has created Brahma, Vishnu, Shiva, goddesses and gods and various other forms.

The fourth lunar day the Lord created the four *Vedas* and four sources of creation and distinction in the forms of speech.
He created eighteen *Puranas*, six *Shashtras* and three qualities. He alone understands the Lord, who instructs himself.

The fifth lunar day, the mortals of five elements are but demons. The Lord himself is incomprehensible and detached.

The sixth lunar day, the Lord has made the six *Shashtras*. The illimitable Lord is known to be apart from them.

The seventh lunar day, if man's body is blessed with chastity and contentment, then all the seven seas within him are filled with the immaculate Name.

The eighth lunar day, he who chastens his intellect does righteous deeds and ponders over the immaculate Lord, obtains the right psychic powers.

The ninth lunar day, the Name is the most powerful Lord of the nine great yogis, the nine regions and all hearts.

The tenth lunar day, contemplate thou the Name, share with others and be pure.

The eleventh lunar day, mortals should enshrine the one Lord in their minds and eschew cruel mindedness, egoism and worldly attachment.

The twelfth lunar day, he whose soul remains detached from the twelve signs, remains wakeful day and night and never sleeps.

The thirtheenth lunar day, mortal man is like a tree on the seashore. But the immortal can become his root, if his mind remains attached to the love of the Lord.

The fourteenth lunar day, the man who enters into the fourth state, who overcomes time and the three qualities of optimism, egotism and pessimism, who lets in the sun of wisdom into the moon's house of darkness and who knows the worth of the way of union with the Lord, he remains absorbed in the love of the Lord, who pervades the 14 worlds, nether land, con-tinents and the solar systems.

The day of no moon is the night the moon remains invisible in the sky.

When the moon rises in the sky its light illumines the three worlds.
*I*st (**838-840**/5/2730-2738)

The Destruction of the World

Ultimately this world shall come to an end and shall merge in him, from whom it has issued forth.
3rd (**1258**/7/4148-9)

2. The World is God's Play or *Maya* (illusion)

Creation comes into being through God's word. Creation and destruction occur at God's behest. Because the world is not permanent and comes to an end at the command of God, it is seen to be temporary and regarded as an illusion (maya), which perishes and is reborn, coming and going again and again. Apart from God nothing is permanent and human beings are puppets in the hands of God. Human relationships are but a passing phase, nobody is a father or a mother to anybody. The whole cosmos is God's play (lila), which he himself has staged.

All sentient beings are thy playthings.
*I*st (**11-12**/1/38)

This world is like a drama staged in a dream, in a moment this play ends.
*I*st (**18**/1/58)

Thou thyself pervadest everything, thou performest wondrous plays.
3rd (**84**/1/282)

Serf Nanak is a sacrifice unto thee. Obviously manifest is thy entire play, O my master.
5th (**97**/1/324)

Besides thee there is no other, no second. The entire universe is the arena of thy play.
5th (**103**/1/343)

The creation and flood occur through the Lord's word. Through the word the creation evolves again.
3rd (**117**/1/387)

The great illusion (*maya*) is the origin of gods and goddesses; through this were created ceremonial treatises (S*mritis*) and schools of philosophy (S*hastras*).
3rd (**129**/1/427)

Searching and seeking, I have seen, O Nanak, that the world is a mansion of smoke.
Ist (**138**/1/456)

Thou who hast made it, understandest it; it is all thy play.
Ist (**138**/1/457)

This world is illusion. It perishes, is reborn, comes and goes.
2nd (**138-9**/1/459)

False is the world but few understand this.
Ist (**147**/1/491)

My Lord God himself creates the world and plays himself in many a way.
4th (**174**/2/582)

What can the poor wooden puppet do? As is the dress the puppeteer clothes the puppet with, so is the part which that puppet plays.
5th (**206**/2/684)

Apart from God's name nothing is permanent. This world is but a play.
3rd (**246**/2/813)

Of his dramas he himself is the actor; he exhibits play and infinite are his pleasures.
5th (**279**/2/928)

He himself is the doer of his play. Who else can speak or deliberate upon it?
5th (**280-1**/2/934)

The Lord himself performs plays, recreations and frolics. He himself enjoys pleasures and yet remains uncontaminated.
5th (**292**/2/973)

The soul, O body, thinking thyself immortal, thou livest in peace, but this world is a play ... Our soul and body are his capital. He himself kills and re-animates.
Ist (**154-5**/2/517)

Wonderful is my master, wonderful is my beloved, wonderful is my Lord God. He himself creates Krishna, and God himself becomes a *gopi* (the milkmaid), the seeker.
4th (**174**/2/581)

When it pleases him, then does he create the world. By his pleasure he absorbs it in himself.
5th (**292**/2/973)

He has made coming and going like a play. He has rendered mammon subservient to him.
5th (**294**/2/981)

He himself has created all men and women. God plays every play.
4th (**304**/2/1016)

Nanak knows not thy wondrous plays.
Ist (**356**/3/1189)

No one is anyone's son, nor is anyone one's mother. Through false worldly love man wanders in delusion.
Ist (**357**/3/1191)

All sentient beings are thy playthings.
4th (**365**/3/1217)

The Lord himself dies and kills himself too. God himself creates and having established, disestablishes.
Ist (**413**/3/1370)

This world's play is fashioned like the mimicry of a buffoon. For a moment in a trice one sees the show. It takes no time to disappear.
Ist (**422**/3/1401)

He of himself creates, and of himself he again destroys; the Lord himself acts and causes others to act. With whom should I lodge a complaint?
2nd (**475**/3/1601-2)

The imperishable Lord has staged this play. It is through the Guru that one understands it.
Ist (**946**/6/3099)

Praise thou the Lord, who having created the world play also beholds it.
Ist (**989**/6/3241)

His mammon he has spread himself and he himself is the beholder of it. He assumes many forms and plays, yet he remains distinct from them all.
9th (**537**/4/1768)

Doubt and delusion are thy creation.
Ist (**537**/4/1863)

For whom should we wail, O father, when this world is but a play.
Ist (**580**/4/1905)

Thou thyself hast constructed the play and thou hast attuned it.
4th (**642**/4/2108)

Thousands are thy eyes, yet thou hast no eye. Thousands are thy forms, yet thou hast not even one. Thousands are thy pure feet, yet thou hast not one foot. Thousands are thy noses and yet thou art without a nose. I am bewitched by these plays of thine.
Ist (**663**/4/2174)

As an actor stages a play and appears in many characters and

guises, so when the Lord abandons his guise and ends his play, he remains alone, the one and only.
5th (**736**/5/2400)

The Lord has made this world an arena for the milkmaids' dance. Creating the stage, he has placed the entire creation within it. In various ways he has made infinite forms and colours. The Lord cheerfully beholds his play and is not tired of beholding it.
5th (**746**/5/2432)

The play of the world is evil. Mortals are sometimes sad and sometimes happy. Of himself the Lord stages the whole play.
5th (**1020**/6/3343)

Everywhere the Lord has staged the play giving breath to the beings. Withdrawing his might, he makes the beings fall.
*I*st (**1033**/6/3389)

The Lord himself knows men's actions and he himself assays them. The entire world is all his play.
*I*st (**1040**/6/3414)

My true Lord has staged a play. He has created no one like another.
3rd (**1056**/6/3471)

All the play and show are the manifestation of thy glory, O God. The true Lord himself creates all distinctions and he himself breaks and builds. The juggler has staged the play. Through the perfect Guru one sees it.
3rd (**1061**/6/3490)

Coming and going is all a wondrous play of thine, O Lord. In creating the creation, thou seest thy beautiful play.
5th (**1077**/6/3542)

Thou, O Lord, art our father and we are all thy children. As thou makest us play, so we play.
5th (**1081**/6/3555-6)

Nanak's Lord is all by himself, standing aloof, he enacts and sees his wondrous plays.
5th (**1082**/6/3558)

The great God has kept air, water and fire within bounds, and has displayed the world play.
*I*st (**1113**/7/3665)

All by himself is the Lord. All that is seen is his own play.
5th (**1204**/7/3969)

In myriads of ways, God the king plays.
5th (**1236**/7/4074)

The whole world is like the game
in a dream. The Lord himself
causes the whole game and play
to be played.
4th (**1311/8/4325**)

Some rare person understands
this, that the creator himself plays
all the games.
*I*st (**1330/8/4387**)

4

KARMA AND TRANSMIGRATION

A. Karma

Introduction

1. Destiny, good fortune and good luck

2. God's judgement concerning past deeds cannot be erased

3. Judgement according to deeds

4. God, the Name, the Guru and the society of saints

B. Transmigration

A. Karma

Introduction

The doctrine of Karma in Sikhism is similar to the doctrine of Karma in Hinduism. Man's present status (good or bad) is determined by his past deeds. He will be judged according to his deeds. If he fails to obtain salvation through good deeds and recourse to the name by the Guru's grace, he will fall back into the cycle of births and rebirths 84 lakh times (=8,400,000). This cycle of births and rebirths can only be broken through the utterance of the name by the help of the true Guru.

According to Hindu belief it is said that creation consists of 84 Lakh (1 lakh = 100,000) Jivas: 9 lakhs in water, 10 lakhs in the air, 20 lakhs in trees and vegetation, 11 lakhs as insects, 30 lakhs as animals and 4 lakhs as humans.

The Karma theory has been very difficult to understand and it raises some questions even in the minds of the Gurus. Since it is God not man who is the doer of actions, how can a poor helpless person be held responsible for the deeds which he has not done?

If man is predestined by God on the basis of his past deeds and he has to act according to God's writ, then how can man be held responsible for his actions in this life, which must conform to God's predictions? What chance does man have of doing good deeds and being saved?

Because of the above mentioned difficulties, the Gurus themselves have felt a deep sense of help-lessness and have asked basic questions, such as the following:

When there was no creation, what did the mortal do then and what deeds account for his birth ...?
5th (**748**/5/2439)

The Lord himself has misled them and put them on the evil track, nothing lies in their power ... Thus says Nanak, what can the poor creatures do, when thou misleadest them into doubt?
3rd (**441**/3/1456)

He is fascinated by mammon. What can the helpless creature do, when the Lord himself causes him to stray?
5th (**707**/4/2314)

When thou thyself causest me to stray, to whom should I go to complain?
Ist (**1188**/7/3915)

Says Nanak, what can the poor creatures do, when thou misleadest them into doubt?
3rd (**441**/3/1456)

Sin and virtue are not under my control.
5th (**899/6/2929**)

1. Destiny, good fortune and good luck

The holy Granth reiterates repeatedly that God records each person's destiny at birth on the basis of his or her past deeds. Human beings act according to God's writ, therefore their chances of attaining salvation are conditioned by their destiny, as they must act according to their prescribed destiny. The name and the Guru and the society of saints are only found with the greatest good luck and good fortune, as recorded on man's forehead by God himself. The scope for salvation thus narrows to the special grace or mercy of God, which can in some cases supersede his own unalterable writ.

Definitions of some key terms:

God's writ :

The command of God written on each person's forehead at birth, concerning their future destiny and salvation on the basis of their past karma.

Good luck & good fortune:

The terms good luck and good fortune are interchangeable and carry a similar meaning for those persons who have been blessed with a favourable destiny written on their foreheads, though it is based on their previous deeds or karma.

They who are pre-ordained by God the creator, by the Guru's instruction get absorbed in the name.
3rd (**65**/1/222)

It is through good luck that the Guru is met.
3rd (**65**/1/223)

By great good fortune, man receives the name.
3rd (**68-9**/1/234)

Great agony befalls deserted brides, who do not possess good fortune .... What deeds have the beloved brides done? They have obtained the fruit of pre-ordained writ.
*I*st (**72**/1/244)

Such destiny shall befall mortal man, as God's pen has recorded on his brow.
*I*st (**74-75**/1/253)

Those who have good luck recorded on their brow, enjoy God's love, O Nanak!
5th (**81**/1/273)

In the Guru's sanctuary God is found, O my trader friend. By greatest good luck; he is obtained.
4th (**81-2**/1/275)

They who bear pre-ordained writ on their brow, O slave Nanak, remember the name of the Lord God.
4th (**82**/1/276)

By great good luck the Guru is obtained and through the Guru's instruction one is ferried across the world ocean.
4th (**82**/1/276)

They who are so pre-ordained come to the Guru and meet him.
4th (**82**/1/277)

Through perfect good fortune, the true Guru, the giver of peace is met and the name comes to abide in man's mind.
3rd (**85-6**/1/288)

The mortal man who has good fortune, pre-ordained on his face and brow grasps and keeps it in his heart.
3rd (**87**/1/294)

He on whose face, the true one has from the very beginning inscribed good luck utters God's name with his mouth.
3rd (**88**/1/296)

Nanak, God's devotion abides within the heart of those, on whose forehead such fate is found inscribed from the very outset.
3rd (**91**/1/307)

By great good fortune, I have pondered over God's name.
4th (**94**/1/315)

By great good luck man finds God's congregation ... without good fortune the guild of the righteous is not found.
4th (**95**/1/318)

Through the greatest good fortune, God has introduced me to his saint ... The unfortunate ones do not obtain the true Guru.
4th (**95**/1/319)

He who has good fortune recorded on his brow obtains the name of the Lord God
5th (**101**/1/335)

O brother, the Lord, in whose home are my treasures, meets him who has pre-natal good actions to his credit.
5th (**108**/1/358)

Taking him by the arm, the Lord merges with himself the one on whose brow the receipt of this gift is recorded.
5th (**109**/1/360)

Unite me with thyself, O true Lord! Through perfect destiny thou art obtained.
3rd (**112**/1/372)

By perfect destiny, God's name is enshrined in man's mind.
3rd (**115**/1/381)

Night and day serve the honourable true Lord. Through perfect good fortune the Guru is obtained.
3rd (**116**/1/385)

I have done the deed which was pre-ordained for me ... without good destiny one does not find the Guru.
3rd (**118**/1/390)

Through perfect good fortune the Guru's service is performed.
3rd (**123-4**/1/409)

The great giver is himself the scribe of destiny.
3rd (**126-7**/1/419)

Nanak, only those persons receive the name on whose forehead such a writ is recorded by the primal Lord.
3rd (**129-30**/1/429)

The creator grants glory to those for whom he has pre-ordained it.
3rd (**130**/1/431)

They, whom thou mercifully protectest through perfect good fortune, merge in thee, O Lord!
3rd (**131-2**/1/436)

In the month of *Jeth* (May), the playful Lord and master meets him, on whose forehead good fortune is recorded.
5th (**134**/1/443)

Serve that true and pure God, who is all powerful, the scribe of destiny.
Ist (**138**/1/457)

Nanak, it is obtained by him on whose face and forehead the writ of good fortune is recorded.
Ist (**147**/1/491)

In the very beginning my Lord God wrote man's full destiny on his forehead.
3rd (**163**/2/545)

On whose forehead it is so written from the very outset, unto them God's name is dear.
3rd (**163**/2/546)

The person within whose mind the Lord dwells swims across. He who has good fortune receives the Lord.
5th (**184**/2/614)

He alone touches the saints' feet, whose fortune is perfect.
5th (**189**/2/630)

Through the greatest good luck the society of saints is obtained.
5th (**189**/2/630)

Through very good fortune, the vision of him is obtained, by him who has enshrined in his mind love for the Lord's name.
5th (**193**/2/642)

In my mortal's lot it was so pre-ordained by the primal being.
5th (**199-200**/2/664)

By great good fortune such a yogi is met, who may cut off the fetters of mammon.
5th (**208**/2/690)

He alone receives the name, who has good fortune recorded on his forehead.
5th (**236**/2/779)

Nanak, greatness is in the true name. Man receives what is pre-destined for him.
3rd (**246**/2/815)

Nanak, he alone knows the Lord, through the Guru, who has good destiny recorded on his forehead.
5th (**251**/2/831)

Through the love of God's name all peace is gained. By great good fortune only a few obtain the name.
5th (**279**/2/927)

The fate of the calumniator is ordained from the beginning.
5th (**280**/2/933)

The vision of the Lord is achieved through the greatest good luck.
3rd (**360**/3/1201)

By the greatest good fortune, I have obtained the God-incarnate, true Guru.
4th (**366**/3/1220)

Through great destiny the detached Lord is attained.
4th (**367**/3/1221)

By good destiny the follower of the Guru obtains God.
4th (**367**/3/1222)

Says Nanak, he who is of perfect good destiny, on meeting the true Guru, obtains the perfect supreme Lord.
5th (**378**/3/1259)

Everything is pre-arranged, what more can be known through de-liberation?
5th (**383**/3/1271)

The saints of the Lord are potent to save. They meet him, who is pre-destined to meet them.
5th (**387**/3/1284)

Enshrining duty and justice in the mind man gains profit. Then one obtains what is written in his lot and stills his ego.
Ist (**420**/3/1392)

Through perfect good fortune a few obtain the name.
3rd (**428**/3/1414)

Without destiny nothing can be obtained. What can we say or do?
3rd (**430**/3/1419A)

The mortal does the deeds which are pre-ordained on his forehead, O my dear.
5th (**432**/3/1425)

They alone meditate on the Lord God's name, on whose forehead it is so written by the primal Lord.
4th (**444**/3/1466)

Those who have such pre-ordained destiny, meditate on God, and their advent (in the world) becomes fruitful and approved.
4th (**445**/3/1467)

They enjoy God's elixir and remain thoroughly detached. Through the greatest good luck they obtain the Lord's ambrosia.
4th (**445**/3/1467)

The men of God, who have attained the society of the true Guru, have on their brow the pre-ordained writ.
4th (**492**/3/1625)

He alone obtains the Lord, O Nanak, who is pre-ordained to meet him.
5th (**501**/3/1652)

O, master, he alone meditates on thee, on whose forehead good fortune is recorded.
5th (**518**/3/1707)

He, on whose brow such destiny is writ comes to bear love for the Guru.
5th (**542**/4/1782)

Without the Lord's writ understanding is not attained. By babbling and prattling man ruin himself.
Ist (**566**/4/1859)

The Lord-incarnate, Sat-Guru comes and meets with those who are so pre-ordained (to meet him).
3rd (**592**/4/1947)

Nanak, remember the Lord's name, through the Guru. By virtue of good luck on one's brow the Lord is attained.
Ist (**598**/4/1967)

The true Guru is ever merciful, O brother, but without good destiny, what can one obtain?
3rd (**602**/4/1977)

Says Nanak, for the one on whose forehead it is so written, disease

is dispelled by meeting with the Guru.
5th (**617**/4/2025)

Says Nanak, he alone obtains it, who is pre-destined to receive it.
5th (**642**/4/2106)

Without God's grace, the name is not obtained. It can be obtained only through perfect destiny.
3rd (**648**/4/2127)

Nanak, through perfect destiny, man meets the true Guru and receives peace, through the four ages.
3rd (**649**/4/2132)

The one who is so destined by God obtains the fruit of the Lord's praise in this age by the Guru's grace.
3rd (**651**/4/2136)

By the greatest good destiny they meet the society of the saints and are regenerated through the Guru.
3rd (**651**/4/2138)

The adepts, the strivers and all men long for the name. But it is through perfect destiny that it is obtained.
3rd (**665**/4/2183)

They who are blessed with high, very high destiny, they alone ponder and reflect on God.
4th (**667**/4/2188)

Some rare one, on whose forehead loving adoration of God is written,

receives the name by the Guru.
4th (**669**/4/2194)

In the society of saints is bliss and peace. Their company is obtained by him on whose forehead such destiny is written.
5th (**676**/4/2217)

My Guru blesses with the name, the man on whose brow good fortune is recorded.
5th (**680**/4/2227)

Nanak, the Lord's slave, whose destiny is so pre-recorded by the creator, has his task accomplished.
5th (**683**/4/2236)

Ill-fated from the beginning are they, who obtain not the vision of the true Guru.
4th (**697**/4/2280)

If the fortunate person's destiny be great, then he will meditate on the Lord God's name.
4th (**880**/6/2866)

The human body is a great ocean, which is filled with diamonds, emeralds, rubies and gems. He who has supreme good luck recorded on his brow excavates and mines them under the Guru's instruction.
4th (**880**/6/2866)

If supremely good destiny is recorded on the forehead, the Lord makes man meet his slaves.
4th (**881**/6/2867)

If I have very good destiny, I shall meet with the Lord's slave, without delay.
4th (**881**/6/2869)

By the Guru's grace, I have heard the divine discourse, which has blessed my mind. Blessed, blessed is my great good destiny.
4th (**882**/6/2872)

As is the pre-destined writ of the creator, so are the deeds we do.
5th (**883**/6/2873)

Thou hast come wandering, wandering, wandering through millions of births. Through the greatest good destiny the society of saints is obtained.
5th (**883**/6/2883)

He who forsakes mammon and associates with the galaxy of saints is emancipated by very good destiny, O Nanak.
5th (**892**/6/2904)

If one has very good luck, then alone does one obtain the Lord's nectar.
5th (**892**/6/2905)

My primal destiny has dawned and after the slumber of many births, I have now awakened.
5th (**892**/6/2906)

My primal and pre-natal destiny has awakened. I ever sing God's praises with my tongue.
5th (**897**/6/2923)

By virtue of primal destiny, I have met with him and he has mercifully blessed me with the Lord's name.
5th (**898**/6/2926)

I am a virtueless sinner, O my Lord. I serve thee not, nor do I good deeds. By great good fortune I have found the Guru's boat.
5th (**913**/6/2978)

They whose destiny thou hast so pre-ordained are attached to thy name, O Lord.
3rd (**917**/6/2990)

This *Gurbani* is enshrined in the minds of those, who are so destined by the primal being.
3rd (**919**/6/2995)

By the Guru's grace, the Lord abides within my mind and I obtain what is pre-destined for me.
3rd (**922**/6/3004)

It pleased the Guru-God to bestow magnificence on *Ramdas*, such was the pre-ordained writ of the Lord's will.
3rd (**924**/6/3011)

They, who have good destiny recorded on their brow, remain satiated, quaffing the name of the earth's sustainer.
5th (**924**/6/3012)

Nanak, he who has such a writ on his brow has all his desires fulfilled.
5th (**927**/6/3021)

The destiny-scribe blesses us with soul and body.
Ist (**931**/6/3034)

Led astray by doubt, men have become crazy. What can they obtain without destiny?
Ist (**935**/6/3052-3)

Wealth is obtained according to past writ.
Ist (**937**/6/3059)

The holy man is the bridge built by God the destiny-scribe.
Ist (**942**/6/3080)

Nanak, he acts as is pre-ordained for him. He cannot act otherwise.
3rd (**947**/6/3100)

However much man may wish, he does not attain to the Guru, unless he is so destined.
3rd (**950**/6/3111)

The one God is the Lord of all. It is through perfect destiny that he is obtained.
Ist (**952**/6/3118)

My mind's aspirations are fulfilled and I have attained to the pre-ordained union with God.
5th (**959**/6/3142)

He alone is blessed with the dust of the saint's feet, on whose brow good fortune is recorded.
5th (**959**/6/3143)

They, for whom there is such a pre-ordained writ, embrace affec-

tion for the formless Lord.
5th (**959**/6/3145)

O, slave Nanak, the Sikh on whose brow good destiny is writ from the very beginning alone comes to the Guru.
5th (**960**/6/3147)

Nanak, he, on whose forehead there is such a pre-ordained writ, loves the true Guru.
5th (**960**/6/3148-9)

He alone, on whose forehead good destiny is writ, takes to the service of the Lord.
5th (**964**/6/3163)

He, in whose destiny it is so writ, O slave Nanak, is blessed by the true Guru with the ambrosial name.
5th (**965**/6/3166)

Be thou dedicated unto thy God, in accordance with the writ pre-ordained for thee.
4th (**978**/6/3204)

Such is the Lord's pre-ordained writ upon my brow, that by the Guru's instruction, I have now come to embrace affection for my Lord.
4th (**985**/6/3227)

They who bear such a writ on their forehead, meet with my flower-girt Lord.
4th (**985**/6/23229)

I have enjoyed my revelries and so my miseries have flowered, such was the primal writ, O my mother.
Ist (**989**/6/3241)

Man obtains what is pre-destined for him. With thy tongue utter the Lord's name, O Nanak! ... He alone is blessed with the name, O Nanak, on whose forehead good fortune is recorded.
Ist (**990**/6/3245)

The light of God, the life of the world is all-pervading everywhere and on every forehead is the true Lord's writ.
Ist (**991**/6/3250)

Through great good fortune and by virtue of the primal writ, I have obtained my Guru, O mother.
3rd (**994**/6/3256)

They alone, who are pre-destined, are blessed with this wealth.
3rd (**1092**/6/3593)

That Lord, contemplate not. It is not writ in thy destiny.
5th (**1093**/6/3599)

They for whom it is so writ by the primal Lord practise his truth.
5th (**1093**/6/3599)

They, on whose brow good destiny is recorded, obtain the shelter of their master.
5th (**1096**/6/3608)

Good destiny is recorded on the forehead of the mate, who enjoys my friend.
5th (**1097**/6/3612)

Wandering and flying, the fly comes near the wet lump of molasses. Whosoever sits thereon is caught. She alone is saved, who has good luck recorded on her forehead.
5th (**1097**/6/3612)

Without destiny, the Lord is not attained and without the true Guru, the mind is not yoked with him.
5th (**1098**/6/3615)

The one who has gone astray, on whose forehead good destiny is pre-ordained, takes to the right path.
5th (**1099**/6/3618)

The Lord becomes manifest unto him, on whose forehead it is so writ, O Nanak.
5th (**1099**/6/3618-9)

When destiny awakens, one obtains the Guru and through him meets the Lord and master.
5th (**1099**/6/3619)

Compassion, righteousness and the Lord's service are eternal. He alone obtains them, in whose destiny it is so writ.
5th (**1101**/6/3626)

The mortal does the deed which the creator Lord makes him do. Even if thou dost run in hundreds

of directions, O man, thou shalt obtain, what thou art pre-ordained to have. Without destiny, thou shalt obtain nothing, even if thou roamest the entire world.
5th (**1102**/6/3630)

Mortal man does the very deed which is pre-ordained by the Lord.
5th (**1102**/6/3631-2)

Thou art the destiny scribe, perfect Lord. Slave Nanak has sought thy refuge.
5th (**1122**/7/3693)

He on whose forehead good destiny is recorded contemplates within his mind God's name through the Guru's instruction.
Bhairo 4th (**1135**/7/3733-4)

The care-free Lord has pre-ordained my destiny.
5th (**1157**/7/3811)

They who have good destiny writ on their brow are blessed by the Guru with God's name.
3rd (**1172**/7/3862)

The true Lord is the true giver and the destiny scribe. He, whom he loves, he yokes to his name.
3rd (**1234**/7/4068)

They alone, who are so pre-destined, O Nanak, receive the name from the Lord.
3rd (**1259**/7/4153)

As many creatures as the Lord has created, on so many foreheads, he has writ their tasks.
4th (**1263-4**/7/4168)

The Lord of the will writes the destines on the heads of all without pen and ink.
Ist (**1280**/7/4222)

By virtue of the Lord's pre-ordained writ on my brow and forehead, I have enshrined the true Guru's feet within my mind.
*4th (***1294**/8/4272)

The love of God is writ on my brow as its destiny.
4th (**1297**/8/4281)

He who is so pre-destined meets with the true Guru and does not fall into the clutches of death's courier.
He who is blessed with perfect good fortune meets the Lord, through the saints' society.
5th (**1341**/8/4425-6)

With pen in hand the inscrutable Lord writes their destiny on the forehead of all.
5th (**1361**/8/4493)

2. God's judgement concerning past deeds cannot be erased

It is by God's written command that mortals are made high and low and obtain woe or weal. Some through his order receive gifts, others are made to wander in transmigration on the basis of their past deeds. Reviewing their past actions the Lord prescribes blessings and curses for all men. According to deeds done the Lord gives them pain and pleasure. Mortals do such deeds as the creator makes them do. He seeks no other job.
Ist (581/4/1910)

To the western mind this may raise moral questions about God's writ or judgement in the absence of freedom of choice on the part of man. Whatever is predestined, according to the Sikh faith, man must not question the order or bhana *(will) of God and must submit to the unchangeable divine writ. Whether this be good or bad, it is not open to question.*

By his command mortals are made high or low and by his written command they obtain woe and weal. Some obtain gifts through his order and some through his order are made to wander in transmigration for ever. All are subject to his fiat and none is exempt from his fiat.
Ist (1-2/1/2)

Union and separation both regulate the world's business and by destiny one obtains his share.
Ist (6/1/21)

They wander in eighty-four lakhs (8,400,000) of species and in their roaming and rambling become miserable. They act in accordance with the pre-ordained writ, which none is able to erase.
3rd (27/1/92)

The writ of the true Lord runs and there is no eraser of it.
3rd (34/1/115)

He was allowed respite to do meritorious deeds as was the primal writ for him.
4th (77/1/261)

Nanak, the mortal, does what is predestined for him. Nought else can be done.
3rd (84/1/284)

The blind self-willed man understands nothing and practises what is pre-destined for him.
3rd (85-6/1/288)

The writ of the Lord no one can erase. Through the Guru one is emancipated.
5th (109/1/362)

This world has gone astray. Thou thyself hast put it on the wrong track.
3rd (111/1/365)

Nothing can be done by man's doing. In the very beginning their

destiny was recorded. Through the greatest good luck my Lord is met.
5th (**135**/1/447)

The inaccessible Lord with pen in his hand writes man's destiny on his forehead.
5th (**261**/2/867)

O, foolish man, why bewailest thou? Thou shalt obtain what is ordained for thee in thy destiny since the beginning?
5th (**283**/2/941)

Man obtains the cargo which is originally destined for him.
5th (**283**/2/962)

There is no escape from that which the creator himself wrote in the beginning.
4th (**309**/2/1030)

Those whose destiny is so writ are attracted to superstition and world-ly love.
5th (**546**/4/1796)

The Lord gives man his turn of human life according to the deeds done by him.
Ist (**566**/4/1860)

As is the writ and as are his former acts, so is what he obtains.
Ist (**579**/4/1902)

Reviewing their past actions, the true Lord writes woe and weal over all men. According to the deeds done the Lord gives pain and pleasure, which remain with the soul. Mortals do such deeds as the creator makes them do. He seeks no other job.
Ist (**581**/4/1910)

O father, all-naked the mortal comes into the world, subject to the recorded writ of pain and pleasure.
The (destiny) or (marriage) writ which is in accordance with past deeds cannot be altered.
Ist (**582**/4/1913)

O friend (father), weep if someone must weep as the beloved soul is goaded on, bound downward. The written order cannot be erased. The call has come from the Lord's court.
Ist (**582**/4/1913)

Nanak, he acts according to his past actions and no one can erase them.
3rd (**594**/4/1951)

Over the head of all beings is the Lord's writ. There is none who is without this writ.
Ist (**698**/4/1967)

Those and only those deeds does mortal man, which thou hast destined for him.
5th (**610**/4/2005)

Nanak has meditated on the Name, and also obtained what was pre-destined for him.
5th (**629**/4/2063)

The creatures born in this world have their destinies recorded on

their foreheads and everyone bears what is destined for him.
Ist (**634**/4/2082)

According to the past writ, which the creator himself wrote, man must act.
3rd (**643**/4/2109-10)

Nanak, they act in accordance with what is pre-destined for them. None can erase it.
3rd (**643**/4/2111)

Nanak, they alone obtain the Name, in whose destiny it is so written by the Lord from the beginning.
3rd (**644**/4/2112)

Nanak, what can be obtained without God's grace? The mortal earns what is predestined for him.
3rd (**645**/4/2118)

The nose-string is in the master's hands and man's deeds drive him on.
2nd (**653**/4/2144)

Man obtains just the thing which he is predestined to receive.
Ist (**660**/4/2166)

As the man acts, so is he rewarded. As he sows, so he eats.
Ist (**662**/4/2171)

According to thy past deeds, thy destiny is recorded on thy forehead. The writ of past deeds cannot be erased. What do I know, what shall befall me?
Ist (**689**/4/2255)

As the mortal sows, so he reaps. This body is the field of actions.
5th (**706**/4/2310)

As is the command issued by thee and as is thy predestined writ, so are the deeds man does.
4th (**736**/5/2399)

He acts in accordance with his past actions which no one can erase.
3rd (**756**/5/2462)

The Lord himself makes man do good deeds and evil ones. Who can know the worth of the inscrutable Lord?
Ist (**766**/5/2496)

As is the pre-recorded writ, so are the deeds he does.
3rd (**787**/5/2563)

He who slanders these homes is predestined by the creator to be destroyed.
5th (**807**/5/2628-9)

He, on whose forehead good destiny is recorded, is the one in whose mind the one Lord abides. Creating the creation, the Lord himself beholds all. None can erase thy writ, O my Lord.
3rd (**842**/5/2743-4)

Thy past deeds shall leave thee not and the very dreadful minister of death shall seize thee.
5th (**900**/6/2933)

Man obtains what is predestined for him. Why does he blame others?
*I*st (**1009**/6/3307)

One realises not the pangs of birth and death. The writ of past deeds cannot be erased.
*I*st (**1009**/6/3307)

The writ of past births cannot be erased. So whom else should he blame but himself? He ever continues coming and going.
*I*st (**1014**/6/3324)

None can erase the true Lord's writ.
*I*st (**1021**/6/3347)

The record of the past is never erased and the blind man is distressed at death's door.
*I*st (**1029**/6/3373)

Weal and woe are the fruit of the deeds of past births. The beneficent Lord, who blesses us with these, alone knows their mystery.

Whom canst thou blame, O mortal man? Thou art undergoing hard misery for thy own deeds.
*I*st (**1030**/6/3380)

What is preordained for man, that he does. None can erase the order of the primal Lord.
3rd (**1044**/6/3430)

No one is able to erase the record of deeds. By the Guru's gospel one obtains the doors of salvation.
3rd (**1052**/6/3458)

My creator Lord, thou thyself art the maker of the world. None can erase what is writ by thee.
3rd (**1056**/6/3471)

Union and separation are the writ of the creator. By undoing, past deeds cannot be undone.
3rd (**1058**/6/3477)

Hear thou, O Lord, each individual enjoys peace and suffers sorrow as a result of the deeds done in the past. Whatever thou givest that is good.
*I*st (**1107**/7/3645)

His command cannot be erased. Whatever he has written goes with mortal man.
*I*st (**1091**/6/3590)

Whatsoever is predestined, that cannot be erased. Bound by the Lord's will, man does his deeds.
*I*st (**1275**/7/4206)

3. Judgement according to deeds

Judgement after death in the court of the righteous judge will be given according to a person's deeds. Therefore by that judgement some will draw near to him and some will be cast away. Human beings will be called to account for every instant and moment of time and to give account for their actions, even though their weight is as little as a grain of seed or a particle of sand. Men act according to the Lord's decree and wander in accordance with their previous actions. By God's fiat they may chance to behold him and whither he sends them thither they go. Men and lesser animals, whatever they are, are born subject to their past actions. As man sows, so he reaps. Without good deeds heaven cannot be attained
Ist (952/6/3117).

Therefore we can say that according to the Granth justice is administered by God according to one's deeds. If anyone says anything else, his ideas are nothing but prattle.
Ist (1238/7/4080)

They are judged according to their deeds and actions. The Lord him-self is true and true his court.
Ist (7/1/24)

Merits and demerits shall be read in the presence of the righteous judge. According to their respective deeds, some shall be near and some distant from the Lord.
Ist (8/1/28)

By virtue of past actions, I have attained to the love of my eminent Lord; He who was separated from me since long ago, has met me.
5th (79-80/1/269)

Even if he longs greatly for the Lord God and also utters his Name, his past actions cannot be erased.
3rd (65/1/222)

He calls men to account for every instant and moment of time and to account for their actions even if their weight is as little as a grain or a particle.
3rd (127/1/420)

Through falsehood and deceit no one has gained God. Whatever one sows that he eats.
4th (40/1/135)

As he sows, so does he reap. Without virtue human life passes away in vain.
Ist (56/1/191)

Men act according to the Lord's command and wander in accordance with their previous actions. By God's fiat they behold his sight and whither he sends them thither they go.
3rd (66/1/225)

Whatever is recorded on man's brow and whatever he sows, that he reaps.
5th (**134**/1/443)

As the man sows, so he reaps; such is the field of action.
5th (**134**/1/445)

Everyone has to reap the fruit of his own actions and adjust his accounts.
Ist (**473**/3/1563)

The bad and the good, thou knowest all. As man sows, so does he reap.
4th (**735**/5/2397)

Day and night we reap the fruit of our actions. Do not blame another. Thy own actions lead thee astray, O man.
5th (**745**/5/2428)

When there was no creation, what did man do then, and what deeds account for his birth?
5th (**748**/5/2439)

Thou doest the deeds, that shall avail thee not. As thou sowest so shalt thou reap or eat.
5th (**888**/6/2926)

Without good actions, how shalt thou swim across.
Ist (**903**/6/2943)

In God is the mine of all jewels, but one attains them by good deeds alone.
3rd (**949**/6/3108)

Without good deeds heaven is not attained.
Ist (**952**/6/3117)

The accounts of all men are held in the Lord's court and none is saved without good deeds.
Ist (**952**/6/3117)

Through good deeds human birth is obtained and in this life the body enjoys worldly relishes.
Ist (**989**/6/3241)

With every breath and morsel the creator Lord takes care of man and he reaps the fruit of his actions.
5th (**1085**/6/3571)

Whatever man does with his hand, with that hand, he obtains the fruit thereof. Not even an instant or moment's delay is caused.
5th (**1098**/6/3615)

Thy past deeds shall leave thee not and death's dreadful minister shall seize thee.
5th (**900**/6/2933)

The writ of past births cannot be erased. So whom else should he blame but himself? He always continues coming and going.
Ist (**1014**/6/3324)

Weal and woe are the fruit of the deeds of past births. He, the beneficient Lord, who blesses us with these, alone knows their mystery.

Whom canst thou blame, O mortal? Thou art undergoing the hard misery for thine own deeds.
1st (**1033**/6/3380)

Hear thou, O Lord, each individual enjoys peace and suffers sorrow as a result of the deeds done in the past. Whatever thou givest that is good.
Ist (**1107**/7/3645)

The writ of past deeds cannot be erased. They themselves eat what they have sown.
5th (**1183**/7/3900)

His turn comes to everyone. The ripe crop is ever mowed down. An account of every moment and in-stant is taken and the soul has to suffer for good and bad deeds.
Ist (**1110**/7/3657)

Only on one's deeds is justice administered. If somebody says and utters aught else, that is nothing but prattle.
Ist (**1238**/7/4080)

Nanak, what man sows, that he eats. He obtains what the creator has destined for him.
Ist (**1243**/7/4100)

4. God, the Name, the Guru and the society of saints

Salvation in Sikhism is obtained by meeting a true Guru through the society of saints, who then gives the name to the devotee to meditate upon and by this process the manifestation of God comes to stay in the mind, in the tenth gate of the body. Then the devotee merges easily with God, called **sahij-samana** *(easy merger). The problem is that God, the Name, the Guru and the society of saints can only be obtained on the basis of a person's good destiny as recorded by God at birth. Man cannot acquire these through his own initiative, as he is bound by his past deeds. The judgement on past deeds cannot be altered by anybody. The only avenue open for the salvation of a person is God's grace and mercy. Only if God exercises his prerogative to save someone, through casting his merciful glance on them, is there any hope; otherwise the fate of a human being is absolutely sealed.*

How can we be true and how can the veil of untruth be rent? By obeying, O Nanak, the preordained order and will of the Lord.
Ist (**1**/1/1)

By virtue of preordained writ, I have obtained the realm of the Lord's love.
4th (**13**/1/42)

By coming in contact with the invaluable personality of the Guru, man becomes invaluable himself and his light is absorbed in the supreme light. The true Guru comes and meets those, who are so preordained.
3rd (**27**/1/92)

O my soul! meditate on the immaculate Lord God. Those who bear such primal writ upon their brow, by the Guru's grace remain absorbed in the Lord's love.
Ist (**27**/1/93)

By great good fortune I have met the society of saints and attained to God, the seat of eternal bliss.
3rd (**29**/1/99)

The treasure of the Name is inexhaustible, through the greatest good fortune it is attained.
3rd (**29**/1/100)

When destiny awakens, man meets the true Guru through the greatest good fortune. Suffering and superstition are annulled from within and peace is procured.
3rd (**31**/1/106)

Through perfect good fortune the Name dwells in the mortal's mind and he attains to the union of the Lord through the world.
3rd (**33**/1/112)

Through perfect good fortune, he whom the true Guru comes to and meets, obtains the society of saints.
3rd (**35**/1/120)

She who by perfect destiny meets the true Guru, finds her darling spouse and is merged into the true Guru.
3rd (**38**/1/129)

It is through the Guru's grace that God is obtained. It is by good luck that thou gettest him.
5th (**42**/1/143)

The Lord, who wrote thy destiny, if he so write, then thy anguish and anxiety are annulled.
5th (**42**/1/144)

He, whose brow bears such a writ, obtains the Lord's presence through the Guru. They who are so preordained clasp the feet of the true Guru.
5th (**44**/1/149)

He alone receives the jewel of the Name, on whose brow good fortune is inscribed.
5th (**45**/1/152)

By meeting the true Guru my face has become clean and I have received what was preordained for me.
5th (**46**/1/155)

The Lord of the world is the comrade of those who are pre-ordained.
5th (47/1/159)

If good luck be recorded on the forehead, only then does man meditate on the treasure of the Name.
5th (47/1/161)

Greatness is in the creator's hand. Mortals obtain it when pre-ordained.
5th (52/1/176)

He who is so predestined obtains such fruit from the Guru, who grants the wealth of the true Name.
5th (52-53/1/178)

They who are predestined reflect over the Lord's Name.
5th (53/1/179)

By virtue of the preordained destiny on my brow, I have attained the Lord.
4th (732/5/2389)

Within my mind has welled up the music of God, the Lord and master, and by the destiny recorded on my brow, I contemplate the Lord.
4th (774/5/2520)

By great good fortune man obtains the perfect Guru and night and day meditates on the Name.
4th (774/5/2522)

By perfect good fortune, I have obtained the Guru and within my mind he has shown me the treasure of the Name.
3rd (798/5/2601)

By virtue of the writ inscribed on my forehead, I have attained to my Guru and the Lord God is enshrined in my mind.
4th (799/5/2602)

The Name is the support of the slaves of the Lord. For them good fortune is predestined by God.
4th (799/5/2603)

Evil is the destiny of those who have not attained to human life.
4th (844/5/2753)

My mind is in love; when through good destiny shall I meet my perfect groom?
5th (845/5/2755)

Man obtains his Lord and master, the ocean of peace, when awakened, if it is in his destiny.
5th (848/5/2763)

By greatest good fortune I have met with my spouse and by the Guru's grace I have contemplated him.
5th (848/5/2764)

Hearing the Guru's instruction, I have acted thereon, for such a perfect destiny was writ on my forehead by the primal Lord.
4th (849/5/2766)

They in whose destiny it is so writ in the past, they alone are in love with the saints.
3rd (**854**/5/2784)

Everyone serves the one true Lord. It is through the primal good that one meets with him.
3rd (**994**/6/3258)

He alone does the various deeds in whose destiny it is so writ by the Lord.
5th (**1002**/6/3284)

He alone, who has good luck recorded on his brow, recognises the one Lord by meeting with the Guru.
5th (**1004**/6/3288)

The Lord is the only raft in the exceedingly dreadful ocean of the world. He alone attains to him, on whose forehead such a writ is recorded.
5th (**1007**/6/3300)

Through the Lord's name poise and peace well up. Without destiny the wealth of the Lord's name is never gained.
Ist (**1010**/6/3309)

He who is born shall assuredly die, according to the destiny inscribed on his head by the Lord, the king.
Ist (**1032**/6/3386)

Riches, intellect, perfection and knowledge are obtained from the Guru. It is through perfect destiny that one meets with the Guru.
Ist (**1038**/6/3407)

They alone abide in the society of the saints, in whose destiny it is so written by the Lord.
3rd (**1044**/6/3430)

There are some whom the Lord forgives in accordance with the eternal writ.
3rd (**1047**/6/3440)

Only those persons attach themselves to the Name, whom the true Lord attaches. Their mind abides in the Name.
3rd (**1050**/6/3450)

Those to whose mind the true Name is pleasing practise the virtuous deeds predestined.
3rd (**1050**/6/3451)

By perfect destiny the Guru's service is performed. If God's grace be upon a man, then he serves him. They alone are in peace, who are pleasing to thee, O Lord and through perfect destiny they are attached to the Guru's ser-vice.
3rd (**1063**/6/3495)

They who are predestined to be so imbued are now imbued with the Lord's love.
3rd (**1066**/6/3505)

Thou art the peace-giving Lord of all beings. It is through perfect destiny that thou art contemplated.
3rd (**1067**/6/3510)

They who are so preordained by the creator Lord, pass their night and day uttering the Guru's name.
4th (**1069**/6/3517)

By the Guru's grace, the Lord becomes manifest to the persons, who from the beginning have that writ recorded on their forehead.
5th (**1076**/6/3539)

By the Lord's will one is emancipated and by the Lord's will he falls into hell. By the Lord's will he becomes a family man and by the Lord's will his slave.
5th (**1081**/6/3556)

B. Transmigration

Introduction

The Holy Granth gives the following reasons for the transmigration of souls through the cycle of 84 lakh rebirths in many different species:

1. *Attachment to the temporal.*

2. *Pride or egotism called* Haumai *causes the egocentric self to be born and reborn repeatedly.*

3. *The failure to recognise the Lord's Name results in souls departing in shame to die and be reborn.*

4. *Through failing to meet the Sat-Guru (true Guru), the spiritual guide, souls wander on through many births and rebirths.*

5. *Not associating with the congregation of the saints leads people to suffer in many existences.*

6. *Failure to serve the Sat-Guru.*

The entire world is transient, subject to coming and going, the merciful Lord alone is permanent. Men act according to the Lord's command and wander in accordance with their previous actions. Their cycle of births and deaths does not cease and they come and go, again and again.

However, opinion seems to be divided among the Gurus as to who actually dies and goes from one existence to another. Is it man or God himself, as we note from the following passages:

The creator alone is seen to be eternal. All others continue coming and going.
*Ist (*54-55*/1/185)*

The true one is ever permanent, he comes and goes not.
3rd (120-121*/1/399)*

No one dies, nor is capable of dying ... The soul perishes not, it is imperishable ... no one dies or comes and goes.
5th (855/6/2883)

It is the maker who comes and goes to the maker.
5th (862/5/2806)

Secondly, what happens to the rationality of the spirit. Where does rationality go when the human soul enters into another species? What actually transmigrates from one existence to another? The Gurus do not shed much light on this question.

References

Without the name man is knocked about (in transmigration). The love of duality has drowned multitudes of men.
*I*st (**19**/1/63)

Those who through the Guru have not understood God's name are reborn after death and continue coming and going.
*I*st (**19-20**/1/64)

All the world continues coming and going.
*I*st (**26**/1/87)

Through profane love no one meets God, and over and over again he continues coming and going.
3rd (**27**/1/91)

Pernicious avarice abides within (mortals, so their) perverted under-standing and intellect does not recognise the Lord. They wander through eighty-four lakhs of species and in their roaming and rambling become miserable. They act in accordance with preordained writ, which none is able to erase.
3rd (**27**/1/92)

In coming and going, in birth and death, an apostate loses honour.
3rd (**31**/1/105)

Because of the love of another, the bride goes round in the circuit of eighty-four lakh lives.
3rd (**31-2**/1/107)

In pride the world perishes. It dies and is reborn and continues coming and going. The perverse recognise not the Lord's name. They depart in disgrace.
3rd (**33-34**/1/114)

Without meeting the Guru, the spiritual guide, mortals wander tantalizingly about in 8,400,000 existences.
3rd (**38-39**/1/131)

They who have not met the divine true Guru are unfortunate and subject to death. They are goaded into existence over and over again, being made like terrible worms in the dirt.
4th (**40**/1/136)

Crowds of mortals without devotion and the name of God continue coming and going.
5th (**47**/1/160)

He who is engrossed in lust, anger and ego, takes birth again and again.
5th (**50**/1/169)

Having wandered through eighty-four lakh existences thou has obtained precious and scarcely procurable human life.
5th (**50**/1/170)

If I walk about forgetting God's name, I shall continue coming and going over and over again.
Ist (**57**/1/193)

Man regrets his coming and going like the crow visiting a deserted house.
Ist (**58**/1/196)

Without the Lord's name, the world has gone astray and suffers transmigration again and again.
Ist (**58**/1/197)

Man comes, goes and is goaded again into existences. He acts in accordance with his past actions. How can pre-natal writ be obliterated, when the writ is written under the Lord's will?
Ist (**59**/1/202)

Men act according to the Lord's command and wander in accordance with their previous actions.
3rd (**66**/1/225)

They go round in a circuit of eighty-four lakh existences and without the name, obtain not salvation.
3rd (**67-68**/1/230)

Their birth and death cease not. They come and go again and again.
3rd (**68**/1/232)

By meeting the Sat-Guru one is not sent round again and the pain of birth and death is removed.
3rd (**69**/1/234)

Some egocentrics like not the Lord's name. Loaded with chains they are graded into species. They return after repeatedly wandering in eighty-four lakh existences and waste their life in vain.
3rd (**69**/1/235)

Mortals continue wandering through eighty-four lakh existences and without the Guru they do not obtain emancipation.
3rd (**69-70**/1/237)

By virtue of good fortune and good deeds done in the past mortals have come into this world and are now doing deeds to shape their future mode of life.
Ist (**75**/1/255)

How can he who has no virtue within obtain peace? An apostate comes and goes. When the body matures it bends, breaks and perishes. Why take pride in this body, which is subject to coming and going?
Ist (**76**/1/257)

He who associates not with the congregation of the saints suffers pain in many existences.
4th (**77-78**/1/262)

Says Nanak, the devotees look beautiful in the Lord's court, while the self-willed ever wander in transmigration.
4th (**78**/1/263)

They go round in (a cycle of) eighty-four lakh existences and are
ruined through death and birth.
3rd (**88**/1/297)

Having forgotten the primal being, O Nanak! (The creative woman) is born and dies again and again.
5th (**89**/1/299)

Ignorant, blind fools do not perform the service of the true Guru. How will they, then obtain the door of deliverance? They repeatedly die and are reborn, again and again they come to birth. At death's door they suffer.
3rd (**115**/1/382)

Deluded by doubt they wander day and night and lose their life in going and coming.
3rd (**116**/1/383)

He who repeatedly dies and is reborn is without the Guru. The one without the Guru continues coming and going.
3rd (**117**/1/388)

Within the body is egotism and egoism, so the circuit of coming and going does not cease.
3rd (**126**/1/417)

Intoxicated with evil passions he understands nothing and falls into existence again and again.
3rd (**128**/1/423)

The egocentric conducts his affairs in egotism. He loses his entire life in the game of gambling. Within him is the supreme darkness of avarice, so he continues coming and going again and again.
3rd (**130**/1/430-1)

Without God's name they suffer agony in coming and going.
Ist (**144**/1/479)

Without serving the true Guru one does not attain to an abode in peace but is born over and over again.
Ist (**144**/1/480)

The whole world is deceived by deceitful mammon and continues coming and going.
2nd (**147**/1/490)

Through the mind's obstinacy men wander through eighty-four lakh existences and continue coming and going.
3rd (**162**/2/543)

They suffer exceedingly the extreme agony of birth and death and repeatedly die and putrefy in the dirt.
4th (**169**/2/566)

In several births thou wast produced as vegetation, within the eighty-four lakh existences, thou wast made to wander.
5th (**176**/2/588)

To the society of saints he does not draw near. Through eighty-four lakh existences he wanders.
5th (**180**/2/600)

Wandering through many existences in several births, I have suffered torture again and again. By thy grace I have obtained the human body. Now grant me a view of thee, O my God, the king.
5th (**207**/2/687)

In the ego of performing burnt offerings, sacrificial feasts and pilgrimages, sins multiply. Man becomes subject to both hell and heaven and is born again and again. In the realm of *Shiva* and the realms of *Brahma* and *Indra*, no place is ever stable. Without God's service there is no peace. Becoming the worshipper of mammon, man continues coming and going.
5th (**214**/2/708)

Eating and drinking, playing and laughing, I have wandered through many births. Playing and suffering pain in many existences I have come to be born as a human being.
5th (**261**/2/866)

They whom the Lord himself misleads rot and putrefy in existence, O Nanak!
5th (**315**/2/1052)

I have grown weary of wandering through many doors and houses. Innumerable are my births. There is no limit to them. Many became my mothers, fathers, sons and daughters. Again many have been my teachers and disciples.
Ist (**932**/6/3040)

They shall pass through eighty-four lakh existences. This number does not decrease, nor does it soar high.
Ist (**935**/6/3054)

The eighty-four lakh beings repeatedly die and are born. They are yoked to existence over and over again.
5th (**998**/6/3272)

Thou shalt repeatedly be born and die and be born again. Thou shalt suffer much punishment on thy way to the distant country.
5th (**1020**/6/3342)

The mammon worshipper passes through eighty-four lakh species of hell. As he does, so shall he suffer.
Ist (**1028**/6/3371)

The blind and apostate have no understanding. They come and go and repeatedly die and depart. Some there are who come and go and obtain no abode in their own home.
Ist (**1029**/6/3373)

The five demons destroy the body. Mortal man reflects not on the Name. He dies and suffers transmigration.
3rd (**1044**/6/3433)

Dedicating my soul and body, I place them before my God. Asleep for many births, I have now become awake.
5th (**1080**/6/3552)

Without the name, no one is man's friend and comrade; without it millions continue coming and going.
Ist (**1111**/7/3660)

Through sins I have wandered in various species and now have sought thy refuge, O Lord!
4th (**1114**/7/3669)

Without the name one continues coming and going, again and again.
5th (**1156**/7/3806)

He has grown weary of wandering in various species and wanders in them over and over again.
5th (**1223**/7/4031)

Wandering about in millions of births in many ways, he obtains no stability anywhere.
5th (**1224**/7/4032)

Man lives, he lives to die and he dies to be born again ... One cannot count the future and the past. What do I know what I was in the past and what I shall be in future?
Ist (**1238**/7/4081)

He who is without ego and self-conceit is not cast into species.
Ist (**1289**/7/4255)

Forsaking God, all those who are attached to the love of another continue coming and going.
3rd (**1334**/8/4401)

Thou thyself has created coming and going.
Ist (**1342-3**/8/4430)

Man wanders, strays and staggers through eighty-four lakh existences. Without knowing the Guru he is caught in *yama's* noose.
Ist(**1344**/8/4437)

5

THE CONCEPT OF SIN IN THE GRANTH

Introduction

It is rather difficult to find a clear-cut definition of sin in the Granth, though the Gurus prayed for the forgiveness of their sins and admitted that sin separates man from God. *Haumai* is the most commonly used word which can be translated as sin. *Haumai* is associated with ego (self-centred-ness), the natural condition that is inherent in *manmukh* (the self-willed person who disobeys God), as contrasted with *Gurmukh* (one who hears and obeys the Guru's word). It is *Haumai* which, through its wilful attachment to *Maya* (or *Mohini*) produces five evil passions called the demons, *kam* (lust), *krodh* (wrath), *lobh* (greed), *moh* (attachment to worldly things), and *hankar* (pride). These passions in turn result in violence, falsehood and doubt, producing evil deeds (*karma*) that bind *manmukh* (the self-willed person) to the unending cycle of transmigration of the soul, with its suffering and pain through repeated births and deaths.

References

In *Haumai* (pride) man comes, in *Haumai* (pride) he departs;
In *Haumai* (pride) he is born and in *Haumai* (pride) he dies;
In *Haumai* (pride) he gives and in *Haumai* (pride) he takes;
In *Haumai* (pride) he acquires and in *Haumai* (pride) he casts away;
In *Haumai* (pride) he is truthful and in *Haumai* (pride) he lies;
In *Haumai* (pride) he pays regard sometimes to virtue and sometimes to evil.
In *Haumai* (pride) he is ignorant, in *Haumai* (pride) he is wise.
Haumai is a chronic disease.
*I*st (**466**/3/1537-39)

My sins are as innumerable as the water with which the seas and oceans are filled. Show mercy and extend a little pity and float me, a sinking stone.
*I*st (**156**/2/523)

My omnipresent Lord, shatter my shackles of mammon and apply me to the service of thy home.
4th (**166**-7/2/557)

I am a sinner, O my pervading Lord ... Show thy mercy unto me too.
4th (**167**/2/558)

O my meritorious and merciful Lord and master, show compassion unto me and pardon all my sins.
4th (**167**/2/558)

O, the beneficent Lord of the meritless, my mind is engrossed in lust, wrath, avarice and worldly love. Show mercy unto Nanak and bless him with thy name.
5th (**210**/2/695)

I am a sinner without merit, O my master, show goodness unto me.
*I*st (**228**/2/754)

My master, take pity on me, a fool and a sinner, and unite me with the society of the Guru, by clinging to which, I may swim across the sea of life.
5th (**250**/2/826-7)

I am not soiled by only one sin, that I may be washed clean with virtue alone.
*I*st (**356**/3/1189)

I am a sinner, unwise, meritless, masterless, vile, stupid, stone-hearted, of low lineage, entangled in the love of the world and stuck in the filth of doubt and acts of egoism. The idea of death does not enter my mind.
5th (**458**/3/1509)

Bless me, a sinner, with a seat in the saint's place of piety, O Lord.
5th (**518**/3/1709)

Banish from within me, lust, wrath, pride, avarice, worldly love and evil sensual desire. Protect me, O my Lord.
5th (**523**/3/1724)

Hearken to my supplications, O my Lord and master. I am full of millions of sins, nevertheless, I am thy slave.
5th (**547**/4/1798)

Show mercy, O God, and save me by thy grace. I am a sinner, I am a meritless sinner, but all the same, I am thy meek slave.
4th (**575**/4/1888)

O my soul, search thou for such a true Guru, by serving whom the pain of birth and death is dispelled.
3rd (**591**/4/1943)

Prays Nanak, hear O my Lord, save me, the sinking stone. I am a wicked sinner. Thou art my immaculate and formless Lord.
*I*st (**596**/4/1960)

I am meritless, low, friendless, orphaned and sinful. I long for the shelter of the saints. I am drowning in the blind well of domestic love. O Lord, stand by Nanak and save him .... O saints, show me the way by which my self-conceit and ego may be banished.
5th (**610**/4/2005)

Lust, wrath, avarice, falsehood and calumny, from these rescue me, O Lord. From within this mind, dispel these and call me close to thee.
5th (**617/4/2026**)

I, a sinner, am sinking in water like a stone. Be merciful and ferry me across.
3rd (**666/4/2185**)

I am blind, ignorant and absorbed in poisonous sins. How can I walk in the Guru's way?
4th (**667/4/2187-8**)

How many misdeeds of mine should I count? They are innumerable. Countless sins and errors have I committed. Day after day, I always do wrong ... I secretly commit agonising sins, but the Lord is the nearest of the near. Prays Nanak, O Lord, show mercy unto me and pull me out of the whirlpools of the dreadful world ocean.
5th (**704/4/2302**)

I have fallen into the clutches of the one who has bewitched the continents and the world. O my Lord, save this sinful soul of mine by blessing it with thy name.
5th (**745/5/2430**)

My soul is soiled with sins and without the Guru virtues never enter my mind.
Ist (**763/5/2485**)

O God, bless me with the dust of the feet of the perfect Guru that I, the sinner, may be emancipated.
3rd (**772/5/2516**)

A sacrifice am I unto thee, O my Lord! Make me meet the mighty true Guru, that shaking off sins I may utter eulogies concerning thee.
4th (**772/5/2516**)

The Lord is merciful to the meek. Thou ferriest thy devotees across the ocean of the world. Save me a sinner from sins.
4th (**799/5/2602**)

Hide thou my faults, O my Guru God. I, a sinner, have sought refuge at thy feet.
5th (**828/5/2694**)

O Lord, thou art the cherisher of those, who seek thy refuge, save me, a great sinner.
4th (**976/6/3200**)

Through sins, I have wandered in various species and now have sought thy refuge, O Lord. Take pity on me, O master, and save me.
4th (**1114/7/3669**)

My Lord, pull me away from the love of sins and attach my mind to the saint's society.
5th (**1120/7/3687**)

O fearless, immaculate Lord, the man-lion, save me, a sinner and a stone.
4th (**1296/8/4277**)

My Lord, show such mercy unto me, that my sins may be burnt away in an instant.
4th (**1325/8/4374**)

Within me the powerful fire of sins is strongly raging. O my Lord, bless me with the ice-cold word of the Guru, that it may be quenched.
4th (**1325-6/8/4375**)

The egocentrics are deaf and blind. Within them is the fire of desire.
3rd (**1415/8/4675**)

I commit many sins, O Lord, of which there is no limit. O God, mercifully pardon me; I am a sinner and a great offender.
3rd (**1416/8/4680**)

Egocentrics pass their life taking pride in their possessions, saying it is mine, it is mine. They putrefy to death.
3rd (**1416/8/4682**)

Egocentrics are like children and dotards, who in their minds do not cherish the thought of God. They do their deeds in egoism, but all go to the righteous judge.
3rd (**1418/8/4687**)

The perverse person, who performs service, but is attached to the love of another, increases his love of wealth, sons, wife and kinsmen. He shall be called to account in the Lord's court. No one can save him in the end.
4th (**1422-3/8/4703**)

In the minds of mammon worshippers is the malady of ego. These evil persons stray through doubt and ego.
4th (**1424/8/4709**)

6

SALVATION

Introduction

A. Salvation explained

1. Salvation through *Suniyai* or listening to the *Bani*

2. Salvation through *Mannai* or by obeying the *Bani*

3. Salvation through uttering the *Nam*, *Shabad* or *Bani*

4. Salvation through meditation on the Name

5. Salvation through subjective experience of the Name

6. Salvation through the society of saints

B. Permanency of salvation

C. Exclusive claims for peace and salvation by the Gurus

D. The grace of God in the Granth

E. What is the *Nam* (the name of God)?

F. Who gives the *Nam*?

1. Guru gives the *Nam*

2. God gives the *Nam*

G. Who can receive the *Nam*?

  1. One who has such a destiny

  2. One who serves the Guru

H. How the Guru is found

Introduction

Salvation according to the Granth is primarily salvation from the endless cycle of transmigration based on *Karma*. Salvation also means becoming one with God, the creator, called *Param-Jot* (the supreme light). This merger of one's *Jot* (light) with the *Param-Jot* (the supreme light) is made possible by the removal of ignorance, ego and *I-am-ness* through the utterance of *Nam* (the name of God), with the help of the society of saints and the instruction of a divine Guru.

The divine Guru by his grace enshrines the *Nam* (name) in the mind of a devotee, who then meditates upon the name, which is the manifestation of God. By so doing the Lord himself comes to stay in his mind. The place of the Lord's abode in the body is called the *Dasham-Dwar* (the tenth gate). It is there that one begins to hear the celestial music of bliss or *Shabad-Kirtan*. The final realm of salvation is called *Sach-Khand* (the realm of truth), where the formless five realms as given by Guru Nanak are as follows: *Dharam-Khand* (the realm of moral law), *Gian-Khand* (the realm of knowledge), *Saram-Khand* (the realm of effort), *Karam-Khand* (the realm of grace) and *Sach-Khand* (the realm of truth).
Ist (**7-8**/1/24-46)

Salvation is achieved through self-realisation by the process of meditation on the *Nam* (name), which is a subjective or mystical experience, assisted by the Guru. This process destroys *Haumai* (egotism) and purges the mind of all its filth and *I-am-ness*, after which the Lord comes to stay in the mind.

The grace of the personal Guru, as well as the invisible God-Guru, is the prerequisite for achieving salvation, on the basis of service rendered to the Guru (*Guru-Sewa*). The grace of God is bestowed upon the most fortunate ones and not on all, in accordance with God's *Hukam* (order), *Bhana* (will) or *Raza* (will), which is not open to question.

Salvation described

The man who in pain feels not pain, who is not affected by pleasure, love and fear, who deems gold as dust. who utters not dis-praise or praise, who suffers not from greed, worldly love and pride, who remains unaffected by joy or sorrow and who minds not honour or dishonour; he who renounces all hope and yearning, who remains free from desire in the world and who is not touched by lust and wrath; within his mind the Lord abides.
9th (**633**/4/2078-9)

Nanak, by merging with the name of the Lord, one obtains union with God.
3rd (**35**/1/120)

If through the name man rids himself of his ego and *I-am-ness*, then the immaculate name comes to abide in his mind.
Ist (**1342**/8/4429)

Note: There are numerous passages in the Granth which say that the past actions of a person cannot be erased. They cast a shadow on the attainment of salvation which is hard to reconcile. For example:

If he greatly longs for the Lord God and utters his name too, his past actions cannot be erased.
3rd (**66**/1/224)

The Process of salvation

1. There is an ongoing cycle of 84 lakh births and deaths, which evolves on the basis of man's past actions or Karma.

2. God inscribes each person's destiny on their forehead at birth.

3. On the basis of a fortunate destiny, God causes some persons to meet the Guru or the society of saints.

4. Then the Guru, through his grace, grants the Nam to a person who meditates on the Nam, according to the Guru's instruction and sees God in his own mind and merges in him. His light merges with Param-Jot (supreme light) and he hears the celestial music of the blissful realm of Sach-Khand (realm of truth), the abode of the formless.

Note: Nam is not abstract name but the manifestation of the Lord God himself.

A. Salvation explained

1. Salvation through *Suniyai* or listening to the *Bani*

According to the Granth salvation can be achieved by various means, such as suniyai, mannai, shabad, or bani and by meditating upon the name of God.

By hearing God's name, man understands the ways of uniting with the Lord. Simply by hearing the Lord's name, the knowledge of the four religious books, the six schools of philosophy and the twenty-seven ceremonial treatises is acquired. By hearing the Lord's name the merit of bathing at the sixty-eight holy places is imparted. Therefore they who sing or hear his name are all emancipated.

They who sing or hear his name are all emancipated. Let us meditate on him, who did create us.
5th (**104-5**/1/347)

By hearing (God's name) the mortal becomes a perfect person, religious guide, spiritual hero and great yogi.
Ist (**2**/1/5)

By hearing (God's name) the reality of the earth, its (supposed) supporting bull and the heaven is revealed unto mortals.
Ist (**2**/1/5)

By hearkening to (the Lord's name) man comes to have the knowledge of the continents, the worlds and the nether regions.
Ist (**2-3**/1/6)

By hearing (the Lord's name) death cannot touch (torment) mortal man. O Nanak, the devotees ever enjoy happiness. By hearkening to (the master's name) sorrow and sin meet with destruction.
Ist (**2-3**/1/6)

By hearing (the Lord's name) (the status of) God of death, God of creation and God of rain is obtained.

By hearing (God's name) even the evil come to sing the Lord's praises with their mouth.
Ist (**2-3**/1/6)

By hearing (God's name) (the mortal) understands the ways of uniting with the Lord and the body's secrets.
By hearing (the Lord's name the knowledge of) the four religious books, six schools of philosophy and twenty-seven ceremonial treatises is acquired.
Ist (**2-3**/1/6)

Ever blissful are the saints, O Nanak. By hearing (the Lord's name) disease and wickedness are wiped away.
Ist (**3**/1/6)

By hearkening (to the Lord's name) truthfulness, contentment

and divine knowledge are obtained.
By hearing (the Lord's name) the fruit of ablution at the sixty-eight holy places is attained.
Ist (**3**/1/6)

By hearing and constantly reading (God's name) man gains honour.
By hearing (the name) man easily procures the meditation of the Lord.
Ist (**3**/1/7)

By hearing (the Lord's name) man dives deep into the ocean of virtues.
Hearkening (to the Lord's name) renders (the mortal) a scholar, a spiritual guide and a monarch.
Ist (**3**/1/7)

By hearing (the master's name) the blind find their way.
By hearkening (to God's name) the unfathomable Lord becomes fathomable.
Ist (**3**/1/7)

When man hears the Lord's name, he becomes emancipated.
Ist (**1343**/8/4431)

Glorious is the Lord's praise and the Lord's name. Praise is the sublime deed in the dark age.
4th (**1314**/8/4336)

Without the name, whatever other deeds man may do, he ever wastes away in egoism.
4th (**1314**/8/4337)

2. Salvation through *Mannai* or by obeying the *Bani*

A Sikh bhakta can also be saved by believing or obeying the name of God. The believer in God's name meets no obstacle, for at death he departs with honour. One who obeys the word, which the Lord dictates, reaches the door of salvation. A Sikh must act according to his belief, in order to be saved.

The condition of (the mortal) who obeys the Lord cannot be described.
If someone tries to describe it, he repents afterwards.
Ist (**3**/1/7)

There is no paper, pen and scribe with whom to sit and reflect over (write) the state of (God's) obeyer. Such is the name of the immaculate Lord. If someone obeys God, such a solitary being understands the bliss thereof in his very mind.
Ist (**3**/1/7)

By truly believing (in the Lord's name) divine comprehension enters (man's) mind and understanding.
By truly believing (in God's name) the knowledge of all the spheres is acquired.
Ist (**3**/1/8)

The worshipper (of God) suffers no blows on his face, through in-

ner belief (in the Lord's name) (man) does not go to death's minister.
Ist (**3/1/8**)

Such is the stainless name (of God), if someone puts faith in the Lord's name, he shall then understand it within his mind.
Ist (**3/1/8**)

The believer (in God's name) meets no obstruction in the way; the believer in the name departs with honour and renown.
Ist (**3/1/8**)

The name's believer walks not in worldly ways, or ritualistic worldly paths.
The believer (in God's name) has an alliance with righteousness.
Ist (**3/1/8**)

The obeyer (of the Lord's dictates) obtains the door of salvation.
The obeyer (of the Lord's dictates) reforms his kith and kin.
Ist (**3/1/8**)

The obeyer (of the Lord's fiat) saves himself and saves the Sikhs of the Guru.
The obeyer (of the Lord's fiat) goes not a-begging.
Ist (**3/1/9**)

3. Salvation through uttering the *Nam, Shabad* or *Bani*

Uttering or chanting the name of God (Nam), Shabad or Bani is yet another way of salvation for a Sikh. As metal ultimately merges in molten metal, so does a praise-chanter get absorbed in the praiseworthy Lord. The Guru says that with my tongue I will repeat the name of God hundreds of thousands of times, so as to ascend the steps to God, in order to become one with him. This is called Nam Japna.

With each tongue lakhs upon lakhs of times I would repeat the name of the Lord of the world. In this way of the bridegroom, there are ladders, by ascending whose steps, I would become one with him.
Ist (**7/1/23**)

Those who have pondered on the name, and have departed after putting in toil, O Nanak, - their faces shall be bright and many shall be emancipated along with them.
Ist (**8/1/28**)

Emancipated and liberated are they who remember thee, O Lord God. The noose of death is cut for them. As a metal ultimately merges in metal, so does a praise-chanter get absorbed in the praiseworthy Lord.
Ist (**18/1/59**)

Without the name, man is knocked about (in transmigration). The love of duality has drowned multitudes of men.
*I*st (**19**/1/63)

By true service one meets the true Lord and obtains the Guru's instructions. That man becomes immune to birth and death. He neither comes nor goes.
*I*st (**19**/1/63)

Through the mind's obstinacy, the man of intellect is drowned and through the Guru the true man is saved.
*I*st (**20**/1/65)

The mortal man, who by the Guru's instruction conquers his mind obtains salvation and deliverance in his own home.
3rd (**26-27**/1/90)

The true immaculate Lord is met through the instruction of the Guru.
3rd (**27**/1/91)

The service of the true Guru is hard. It is obtained by surrendering one's head and by eliminating self-conceit. If man realises the word, then does he meet God and all his service becomes acceptable.
3rd (**27**/1/92)

Without the Guru, man does not obtain God's mansion, nor does he attain to his name. Search far and obtain such a true Guru through whom thou mayest gain that true Lord.
3rd (**30**/1/103-4)

Nanak, God and the Guru have two forms but they have the same light. It is by the word that man attains to union with God.
3rd (**30**/1/104)

By serving the true Guru man attains to eternal peace and his light merges with the supreme light.
3rd (**31**/1/105)

If by the Guru's instruction man sings the praises of God, he automatically dyes him with his love.
3rd (**32**/1/110)

By meeting the true Guru man is relieved of the bondage of the three qualities and obtains the door of salvation in the fourth state. If man dies with God's name, he is saved then and obtains the door of salvation.
3rd (**33**/1/113)

If mortal man ponders on the name with a pure mind, then he reaches the door of salvation.
3rd (**33-4**/1/114)

If it (he) performs the service of the true Guru and keeps the true being clasped to its (his) heart, it (he) is saved then.
3rd (**34**/1/116)

Through the Guru's hymns God is obtained. Without *Gurbani* man

is lost in doubt.
3rd (**36**/1/122)

Through the true word, God is gained and man remains blended with God.
3rd (**36**/1/126)

They who fall at the Guru's feet are freed from bondage.
3rd (**39**/1/134)

No one can save except the Guru. I see no one else. I have searched all four directions and have come and entered the Guru's sanctuary. I was drowning (but Guru) the true king, has saved me, O Nanak!
5th (**43**/1/146)

Suffering and sorrow do not touch him, who has the support of God's name.
5th (**44**/1/149)

Nanak, it is through the name (*Shabad*) that union with God is effected and separation occurs no more.
*I*st (**56**/1/191)

True is the honourable Lord and true is his *Gurbani*. It is through the word that union with God is effected.
3rd (**64-5**/1/220)

Nanak, the Lord alone is the giver, there is no other second. By the Guru's grace the Lord is obtained and it is through good luck that the Guru is met.
3rd (**65**/1/223)

By eulogising the perfect Guru, the Lord easily meets man.
3rd (**67**/1/229)

By the Guru's grace, I have obtained God.
*I*st (**73**/1/247)

I fall at the Lord's feet to conciliate him. The true Guru has united me with the Lord. There is none so great as he.
*I*st (**73**/1/248)

By practising the name through the Guru, God comes within the mind.
3rd (**67**/1/229)

When they remember the name and when the true Guru unites them with the Lord, then they attain to emancipation.
3rd (**67-8**/1/230)

By granting pardon the perfect Guru unites man with the creator.
3rd (**68**/1/233)

It is from the divine word that poise proceeds and the true God is obtained.
3rd (**68**/1/231)

Through the word God dwells in the mind and the tongue tastes God's nectar.
3rd (**68**/1/232)

The Lord unites to himself even those who stray. It is through the name that union is accomplished.
3rd (**68**/1/233)

By merging man with his name, God unites him in union with himself.
3rd (**69**/1/235)

By the Guru's words, God is obtained and the Lord ferries man across the world ocean.
3rd (**86**/1/290)

Through the Guru, he beholds with his eyes, the unseen, unapproachable, unknowable and immaculate Lord.
3rd (**87-8**/1/295)

They who serve their true Guru cross the terrible ocean.
3rd (**89**/1/300)

The Guru, who himself is the pardoner, wipes out their demerits with merits.
3rd (**90**/1/303)

The perfect Guru has shown my God around me.
4th (**96**/1/321)

By the Guru's grace, I have seen the one Lord. Unto the true Guru, I am a sacrifice.
3rd (**96**/1/321)

God is merciful to the poor, cherisher of the world and master of the universe. By meditating on him under the Guru's guidance salvation is obtained.
5th (**98**/1/327)

Showing his mercy the Guru has united me with the Lord. Through great good luck my

comings and goings have ceased and my hopes have been realised, O Nanak!
5th (**105-6**/1/350)

He who dies with God's name and subdues his mind, obtains the door of salvation.
3rd (**117**/1/386)

The Guru's ward acquires divine knowledge and through God's name gets emancipated.
3rd (**117**/1/387)

Nanak, he, on whom the Lord bestows his name, obtains and treasures it in his heart.
3rd (**124**/1/410)

Nanak, he on whom the Lord casts his merciful glance gains the name. Through his grace the name is enshrined in the heart.
3rd (**126**/1/418)

They who have pondered on the name and have departed after putting in toil, O Nanak, their faces shall be bright and many shall be emancipated along with them.
2nd (**146-7**/1/488)

I ask for thy light, grant it to me, O my beloved. Who has not been saved by serving thee?
5th (**386**/3/1283)

Foolish, stupid, ignorant and thoughtless am I. Thy name is my mind's only hope.
5th (**388**/3/1287)

Reflecting over and accepting the Guru's instructions, the soul hears the heavenly music. By understanding itself the soul becomes the formless Lord.
Ist (**415/3/1378**)

His sins and ills of many births are washed away and he merges in the Lord and master's name.
4th (**445/3/1466**)

Myriads of sins are all destroyed by repeating God's name.
5th (**707/4/2311**)

I utter the name of Lord God, the supreme person, and my poverty and hosts of sins are all destroyed. Through the Guru's hymns my fear of birth and death is removed. Serving the ever constant Lord, I am absorbed in peace.
4th (**731/5/2385**)

The purifier of sinners is thy name, O Lord. Bless thou me thy slave with the gift of thy name.
5th (**898/6/2926**)

He who believes in the name becomes victorious. No other deed is of any account.
Ist (**954/6/3125**)

My comings and goings have ended and my misgiving are removed. Stilling my self-conceit, I have met my Lord and now wear the apparel of truth.
The Guru has rid me of ego, I have renounced (ego) and my sorrows and sufferings are dispelled. My light is merged in the supreme light and I have recognised my own self.
Ist (**1111/7/3659**)

Thy bride's (mine) eyes are brimful with tears. I utter thy praise. How can I meet thee, O my beloved Lord? I know not the arduous way and path to thee. How can I reach thee, O my love, at the yonder shore?
Ist (**1111-1112/7/3659**)

Nanak, when I met with my most darling Guru, my light merged in this supreme light.
Ist (**1112/7/3659**)

Whosoever remains detached and desireless amidst desires and lovingly contemplates his Lord, he is released by the Guru's grace and is attuned to the Lord's name, prays Nanak..
Ist (**1126/7/3704-5**)

Contemplating the Lord's name day and night, I shall not die again. O Nanak, I have ultimately become he, from whom I had issued forth.
5th (**1193/7/3934**)

Immaculate is the Lord God's name. By hearing and uttering God's name, pain departs.
4th (**1316/8/4344**)

Utter ye all with your mouth the name of God, the man-lion ....
Sublime is the profit of meditation on the Lord God.
4th (**1316-7/8/4345**)

The Lord's name pervades and fills all. Utter only the all-pervading name of the Lord.
4th (**1316-7/8/4345**)

Ever utter thou, the Lord's name. Through it, thou shalt be rid of lust, wrath and ego and shalt be attuned to the one Lord.
5th (**1341/8/4425**)

The Lord's name is the purifier of the sinner.
5th (**1323/8/4365**)

By the name, O Lord, man is ferried across (the ocean) and by the name he is honoured and adorned.
Ist (**1327/8/4378**)

Thy name is my strength and thy name my support.
Ist (**1327/8/4379**)

Bereft of the name, bound hand and foot, the world goes to the city of *Yama*.
Ist (**1327/8/4399**)

O Lord, thy name is the gem and thy grace the light. In whichever mind is thy name, there is the divine light.
Ist (**1327/8/4380**)

O, my infinite creator Lord, thy name alone and nothing else is the cure of all ills.
Ist (**1327/8/4380**)

Nanak, through the Lord's name, man is emancipated and rid of the agony of birth and death.
Ist (**1330/8/4389**)

The perfect true Guru has blessed me with the name and I have obtained joy, bliss, emancipation and eternal peace and all my affairs have been adjusted.
5th (**1340/8/4422**)

Without the true Guru, no one is emancipated.
Ist (**1343/8/4433**)

They who utter the Lord's name are emancipated. O Nanak, the very fortunate ones alone are blessed with this state.
5th (**1360/8/4490**)

To forget the Lord of the world is death. To contemplate God's name is life.
5th (**1361/8/4491**)

4. Salvation through meditation on the Name

The true Guru can be met by God's grace and good fortune. He gives the devotee the name. As a result of the service rendered to him through meditation on the name, a Sikh enters the realm of supreme bliss, when the name as the manifestation of God comes to stay in his mind. Therefore the wealth of God's name abides in the mind and he gets absorbed in the celestial bliss and his light merges with the supreme light. This merger is called sahij-samana or easy union with God. Thus transmigration ceases and the enlightened soul no longer continues bound to the wheel of existence.

The name alone saves the world. This alone is my hope and this my mainstay.
*I*st (**24**/1/83)

Meditate on God's name, worship the name and through the name enter the realm of supreme bliss.
3rd (**26**/1/88)

They who have served the true Guru, have obtained the treasure of the name.
Their heart remains saturated with God's elixir and their mental pride is annulled.
3rd (**26**/1/88)

They who possess the inexhaustible name of the infinite Lord, remain happy in the four ages. By meeting the Guru, God's name is obtained and the thirst for worldly love departs, O Nanak! By the Lord's grace the true name is obtained, the treasure of excellence.
3rd (**26**/1/89)

They, who with single mind contemplate God's name and dwell upon the Guru's teaching, their faces are ever bright in the Lord's true court.
3rd (**28**/1/95)

The wayward know not the name, and without God's name they lose their honour. They relish not God's name and are attached to duality.
3rd (**28**/1/95)

Continence, truthfulness and self-restraint are all contained in God's name. Without the name man does not become spotless.
3rd (**34**/1/112)

By performing the service of the Guru, the name is gained and one remains absorbed in the true Lord.
3rd (**34**/1/114)

The wealth of God's name abides within his mind and he gets absorbed in the celestial bliss, O Nanak!
3rd (**34**/1/115)

I submit to the will of the true Guru and have expelled my self-conceit from within me. This is

the service and meditation of the Lord by which the name comes and dwells in my mind.
3rd (**34/1/117**)

This true soul then is dyed in the true name and remains absorbed in the true Lord. In speech, light and utterance this soul remains permeated by the name.
3rd (**35/1/119**)

Nanak, by merging with the name of the Lord, one obtains union with God.
3rd (**35/1/120**)

The Lord unites with himself those, whose souls are fascinated by the true word. Night and day, they remain imbued with God's name and their light is absorbed in the supreme light.
3rd (**35-36/1/120-1**)

Without the name everyone is miserable and is ruined by duality.
3rd (**35-6/1/121**)

Praise the name of the Lord and thou shalt not come and go again.
3rd (**36/1/122**)

O my soul, by being imbued with the name, thou shalt procure peace.
3rd (**38-39/1/131**)

The name, thy helper, is ever with thee and shall save thee hereafter.
5th (**44-5/1/151**)

The mind's desires are fulfilled, when man finds the treasure of the name.
5th (**46/1/155**)

By his grace the Lord has given me his name and united me with himself. The Lord himself has become merciful and my comings and goings have ceased.
5th (**46/1/156**)

Being imbued with the name in his home, mortal man obtains the eternal status of salvation.
Ist (**58/1/196**)

If man forgets not the name, the Guru shall unite him with the creator, O Nanak.
Ist (**59/1/200**)

Without God's name, mortal man cannot be saved. By the Guru's instruction, he is united in union with the Lord.
Ist (**59/1/202**)

The Guru firmly installs God's name with love, but without his embrace man cannot attain to the name.
3rd (**65/1/223**)

Nanak, greatness is in the name of God. By the Lord's favour the name is attained to.
3rd (**66/1/226**)

Through the word one meditates on the name and through the word he gets absorbed in the true one.
3rd (**67/1/227**)

Without the divine word doubt is not dispelled nor does pride depart from within.
Without love the Lord's service cannot be performed and without the name one does not become acceptable.
3rd (67/1/228)

With the name ego is stilled and mammon's illusion departs.
Through the Guru man easily obtains the wealth of God's name.
The Lord easily meets mortals within whose mind the name of God, the lover of devotion, abides.
3rd (69/1/228)

Some egocentrics like not the name. Loaded with chains they are goaded into (existence in) different species.
3rd (69/1/235)

When the true Guru is mightily pleased, the true name is obtained O Nanak!
3rd (71/1/241)

Everyone longs for thy name. Without the true Guru thou art not found.
Ist (71-2/1/243)

Without the name of the all-pervading God, the world is not emancipated and is drowned because of the love of duality.
Ist (75/1/255)

The true Guru has implanted the true name within me and I remain absorbed in the love of the true name. Nanak, the giver of the name is true (Guru) and he is obtained by God's grace.
3rd (84/1/283)

I sang the Lord's name and God's praises. The divine light was kindled and I was shown the way.
3rd (86/1/291)

If the Lord's name dwells in the mind even for an instant, it includes (the merit of) bathing at all the sixty-eight places of pilgrimage.
3rd (87/1/293)

In the true Guru is the treasure of the name, which is obtained by God's grace.
3rd (88/1/297)

By meditating on God's name, mortals become demigods.
3rd (90/1/304)

The true Guru, the bestower, has implanted God's name in my heart. By the greatest good luck I have obtained a sight of the Guru.
4th (96/1/320)

The true Guru has caused me to hear God's name, the treasure of excellence and all my ailments are eliminated.
5th (99/1/336)

God is mine and I am a slave of his, O Nanak! The Guru has given me the true name.
5th (100-1/1/335)

The treasure of the name is obtained by him, in whose mind the Guru's hymns abide.
Whosoever drinks the nectar, he is gratified. He who obtains the nectar of the name becomes immortal.
5th (**101**/1/335)

The saint has given me the medicine of God's name. It has cut off my sins and I have become pure .... Happiness reigns all around. My pains have all departed and all my pangs are over. With every breath of his, Nanak sings the praises of God. The true Guru has screened (hidden) my sins.
5th (**101**/1/337)

The nectar of the name is ever the peace giver. By the Guru's instruction it abides in man's mind.
5th (**109**/1/361)

True is the Lord and true his name. By the Guru's grace, I place him in my mind.
3rd (**110**/1/364)

He, on whom the master casts his merciful glances, obtains his name. By the Guru's grace, his egotism departs. He, within whose mind God's name abides, obtains honour in the true court, O Nanak.
3rd (**114-5**/1/379)

Without the Guru the name cannot be obtained. The perfect people and the strivers miss it and bewail. Without serving the Guru peace is not produced. Through perfect good fortune the Guru is obtained.
3rd (**115**/1/380)

Without the Sat-Guru, God cannot in any way be seen. By showering his benedictions on me, the Guru has shown me the Lord.
3rd (**115**/1/380)

The true Guru, the giver, is met, when God causes man to meet him. By perfect destiny, God's name is enshrined in man's mind. The greatness of God's name is obtained by chanting the excellences of the true Lord, O Nanak.
3rd (**115**/1/381)

Without God's name all are deluded by doubt. From the Guru's service God's name is obtained. Without the true Guru, no one can receive the Lord's name.
3rd (**116**/1/383)

The Lord himself grants pardon and unites the soul with himself. From the perfect Guru man obtains the treasure of the name. By dwelling on the true name the soul is sanctified, and by serving the true one sorrow is driven away.
3rd (**116**/1/385)

The Lord himself summons and bestows his name.
3rd (**117-8**/1/389)

When the immaculate name is enshrined in the mind, the body

and soul are rendered pure and the love of mammon departs. He who ever sings the pure praises of the true Lord, in him the holy celestial strain resounds.
3rd (121/1/400)

By perfect good destiny they attain to the Guru, who through the name, unites them with the Lord.
3rd (122/1/405)

The true Lord is free of care. By the Guru's gospel the name abides within the mind and man gets united with God, O Nanak.
3rd (122-3/1/406)

Without the Lord's name there is darkness within. One does not receive the real and the round (of birth and death) does not end. In the true Guru's hand is the key, none else can open the door. By perfect good luck the Guru is met.
3rd (124/1/412)

When it pleases him, then the Lord merges the mortal with himself.
3rd (128/1/424)

He who created the world knows everything about it. The Lord merges with himself those who ever keep the Guru's instructions in view.
3rd (129-130/1/429)

O Nanak, by praising the true name, I have obtained the perfect Lord.
Ist (150/1/504)

The Lord's name always gives peace.
9th (1008/6/3302)

God's name is as meritorious as the sixty-eight holy places of pilgrimage and is the destroyer of sins.
Ist (1008/6/3304)

Searching the home of his body according to the Guru's instruction, he obtains the wealth of the Lord's name .... Imbued with meditation on the name, *Brahma, Vishnu* and *Shiva* became sublime.
Ist (1013/6/3321)

All the comforts of emancipation are contained in meditation on the name and the *Gurbani*. So I enshrine the true name within my mind.
By the Guru's grace, the immaculate name of the Lord is obtained and the unendurable load of sins is removed.
Ist (1013/6/3322)

Emancipation and salvation stand at the door of the saint, in whose mind is the treasure of the name.
5th (1017/6/3334)

Pain, agony and trouble are eradicated in the mind of the one in whom the Lord abides. Death, hell, agonising abodes and sins touch him not.
5th (1017/6/3334)

The five demons destroy the body. Mortal man reflects not on

the name. He dies and suffers transmigration.
3rd (**1045**/6/3433)

Through the true name, one obtains true honour. Without the name, no one attains emancipation. Without the true Guru, no one finds the name. Such is the rule which my Lord has established.
3rd (**1046**/6/3436)

By the Guru's grace the true name is recognised. He has no family nor has he a mother.
3rd (**1051**/6/3452)

Without the Lord's name the gyration of transmigration never ends ... He on whom the Lord has mercy obtains God and the true name comes to abide in his mind.
3rd (**1052**/6/3456)

Ever peace-giving is the name of the incarnate Lord. It is through the name that one earns profit. Without the name, there is only misery in the world. The more evil deeds one does, the more one's sins become.
3rd (**1052**/6/3491)

Only that man is emancipated who dies through the name. The name then abides within his mind and he meditates on the name of the worthy Lord, O Nanak ...
Without serving the true Guru, one is never emancipated. Let anyone enquire from divines and contemplatives.
3rd (**1052**/6/3496)

Without the name, all is utter darkness. Rare is the one who understands this through the Guru's grace.
3rd (**1065**/6/3501)

Nanak makes a supplication, it is through the name that one merges in the Lord, the name incarnate.
3rd (**1068**/6/3511)

Through the name one's comings and goings are ended and one keeps the true name enshrined in one's mind.
3rd (**1068**/6/3512)

Through the name, man's mind is illumined, he abides in peace and his light blends with the supreme light.
If man serves the true Guru then he is emancipated and overcomes the five demons.
3rd (**1068**/6/3513)

By the Guru's grace, one obtains the wealth of the name. When the Lord showers his benedictions on me, he blesses with his name and Nanak merges in the name.
4th (**1069**/6/3517)

By the Guru's grace, they utter and repeat the name of God.
4th (**1069**/6/3518)

Without the name, no one is man's friend and comrade. Without it millions continue coming and going.
1st (**1111**/7/3660)

If thou, O Lord, showest mercy and savest me then alone can I be saved. O compassionate to the poor, bless me with thy true name.
Ist (**1112**/7/3660)

By the Guru's grace, lovingly utter the Lord's name with thy tongue. In this way thou shalt cross the world stream.
Ist (**1126**/7/3704)

The Lord's name, which is the wealth and support of all, is obtained in the mind by the Guru's grace.
Ist (**1127**/7/3704)

Without the Lord's name, no one obtains salvation and all are drowned without water ....
Though man may give gratuitous feasts, make burnt offerings, offer alms, perform penance and worship, and constantly endure bodily pain and suffering, yet without the Lord's name, he cannot obtain emancipation and the redeeming name, which one receives by the Guru's grace.
Ist (**1127**/7/3704)

Through the Guru's instruction, serf Nanak has ob-tained the name and by contem-plating the Lord and master he is emancipated.
4th (**1136**/7/3737-8)

In the dark age, one is emancipated only through the name. Nanak utters the name of the creator Lord.
5th (**1138**/7/3744)

Nanak is redeemed through the name's act of atonement.
5th (**1142**/7/3760)

Unfathomable, unweighable and supremely priceless is the treasure of this name. The name is my immovable master.
5th (**1144**/7/3765)

He alone receives the name, to whom the Lord gives it.
5th (**1148**/7/3781)

Associating with the saintly Guru, miseries and maladies are ended. So servant Nanak has easily met his God, the spouse.
Ist (**1170**/7/3854)

By giving the gift of God's name, the Guru unites man in union with God.
Ist (**1170**/7/3855)

Without the name, no one obtains emancipation.
3rd (**1175**/7/3872)

Contemplating the name, one is emancipated. Contemplating the name one attains sublime peace and praise.
5th (**1181**/7/3891)

Emancipate thou me, O my merciful master.
5th (**1181**/7/3894)

With the true Guru's word, my mind is satisfied and I have obtained God, the support of my vital

breath.
Ist (**1197**/7/3948)

The supreme Guru's word is the Lord's name and this name I enshrine in my mind.
(Note: There is no word for "supreme" in the original. The word is "Gurmukhi-Bani", which means "the Guru's word".)
2nd (**1239**/7/4083)

Mine eyes incessantly gaze upon my Lord and master. Seeing the true Guru, my soul has blossomed and I, the slave, have met with my Lord, the creator.

O Lord God, unite me with the Guru-saint, who day and night keeps God clasped to his heart.
4th (**1262-63**/7/4165)

Slave Nanak has obtained his Lord, the destroyer of all poverty and pain and through his name, he is emancipated.
4th (**1294**/8/4272)

5. Salvation through subjective experience of the Name

This is not much different from meditation on the name, except that salvation is not to be sought outside the body and the mind. It is by pondering on God and deliberating on him in the mind that saints get peace in this world and the next. There is darkness within the mind of the deluded. This ignorance has to be removed by self-realisation. The Guru helps through the name to explore the realm of the Lord within the mind. Everything is within and nothing is without; he who seeks for God outside is lost. By the Guru's help one can find God within oneself in the mind, as God comes to stay in the mind, in the tenth gate, or Dasham Dwar. As the waves blend with the sea, so one's light blends with the Lord's light, when divine light dawns and dispels the darkness of ignorance. By the Guru's grace man obtains the true Lord. Within his mind and body he beholds him and the evil of egoism departs. He who closes his nine doors and restrains the wandering mind, obtains an abode in the Lord's tenth home. There the unstruck music plays day and night. Through the Guru's instruction this celestial music is heard.

Within them is the name treasure and through the name they are renowned. They worship God's name and believe in nothing but the name.
*I*st (**17**/1/54)

Solace accrues when he, who is the owner of life and soul, abides in (man's) mind.
*I*st (**18**/1/58)

In the mind are the emeralds, rubies, pearls, valuables and jewels of God's name. True merchandise and wealth is the name of the infinitely profound Lord, who permeates all hearts.
*I*st (**22**/1/74)

Within man are all the goods. From within his home he can obtain the required merchandise. Every moment remember God's name.
3rd (**29**/1/100)

The treasure of the name is inexhaustible, through the greatest good luck it is attained to.
3rd (**29**/1/100)

By pondering and deliberating in their mind on God the enemy of ego, they obtain peace in this world and the next.
In their own house they get to the Lord's presence by reflecting on the Guru's words.
3rd (**30**/1/101)

Serve the true Lord who will grant thee true greatness. By the Guru's grace, God abides within man's mind and drives away his pride.
3rd (**30**/1/101-2)

When the treasure of the name ever abides in man's mind, he finds a place in Lord's abode.
There is darkness within the body and mind of an apostate. He has neither shelter nor place of rest. He continues roaming about in many existences, like a crow in a deserted house.
3rd (**30**/1/102)

In the three temperaments is the attachment of wealth. The Guru's beloved attains to the fourth state of celestial beatitude. The Lord mercifully unites with himself, those within whose mind God's name has entered and abides.
3rd (**30**/1/103)

Through perfect good fortune the name dwells in the mortal's mind and he attains to union with the Lord through the word. The name of God comes and abides in the mind of him, who under the Guru's instruction remains dead while alive.
3rd (**33**/1/112)

Within thee God abides. Do thou attain to peace by serving the Guru.
3rd (**33**/1/114)

They who recognise their own self, find the Lord's mansion in

the good place of the home of their heart.
Ist (**56-7**/1/192)

In the body are the shops, cities and fortresses, wherein the merchandise of the true name can be traded.
Ist (**57**/1/194)

Who except the Guru can explain that God, the king and emperor, abides within man's mind.
Ist (**61**/1/207)

Men ruin themselves by their search without, while the thing (they seek) is in the sacred place of their home. The pious receive it in their lap, whilst the perverse miss it through the ego.
Ist (**63**/1/214)

By practising the name through the Guru, God comes and dwells within the mind.
3rd (**67**/1/229)

By meeting the perfect true Guru, God comes and dwells in man's mind and heart.
4th (**82**/1/277)

The foolish and ignorant man recognises not the creator, who is within his self. Because of the love of duality, he who instructs the world and himself understands not divine knowledge.
3rd (**86**/1/289)

Everything is within the home, not even one is without. He who seeks without, is lost in doubt. By

the Guru's grace, he who has found the Lord in his mind is comfortable within and without.
5th (**102**/1/338)

As the waves blend with water, so my light blends with the Lord's light.
5th (**102**/1/339)

If man searches his body and soul, then he finds God's name. He restrains his wandering mind and keeps it under control. In the body are countless articles. Through the Guru, if I attain to the truth, then alone can I see them..
3rd (**110**/1/363)

Within mortal man jewels and rubies are produced. By the Guru's instruction, man tests them and gets them tested.
3rd (**112**/1/371)

Within mortal man is the jewel of the name. It is obtained if the Guru makes it accessible. Otherwise the mind is engrossed in the three qualities of mammon (*maya*).
3rd (**117**/1/386)

Only within is the thing, but the fool searches for it without. The blind apostates roam about like demons. Where there is the thing, from there no one obtains it. The wayward are gone astray in doubt.
3rd (**117-8**/1/389)

Nanak, the Lord's name abides within his mind. He unto whom

the Lord donates his name attains to it. By enshrining in the heart the nectar of the name of God, all pain of egotism and egoism is eliminated.
3rd (**118**/1/391)

My master by sitting in men's minds beholds their actions. The person who by the Guru's grace meets God is on that account (accepted).
3rd (**123**/1/408)

Within the cavern of this body there is inexhaustible treasure. In it abides the unseen and illimitable Lord. He himself is unmanifested and manifest. By the Guru's instruction self-conceit is effaced.
3rd (**124**/1/410)

The Guru has applied to mine eyes the true salve of divine knowledge. Within my mind the divine light has dawned and the darkness of ignorance is dispelled. My light has merged with the divine light, my mind is propitiated and I am blessed with glory in God's court. ... If someone goes beyond his body in search of the Lord, he receives not the name but suffers the great misery of forced labour. The blind perverse person realises not, but when he again returns home, through the Guru, he finds the real thing within.
By the Guru's grace man obtains the true Lord. Within his mind and body he beholds him and the filth of ego departs. Sitting in the

sublime place he always sings God's praises and is absorbed in the true Lord.
He who closes his nine doors and restrains his wandering mind, obtains an abode in the Lord's tenth home. There the unstruck music plays day and night. Through the Guru's instruction this celestial strain is heard.
3rd (**124**/1/411)

By the Guru's grace, I have found him in my own home.
3rd (**126**/1/416)

Within man's mind is the light of him, whose expanse is manifest. By the Guru's instruction the darkness is dispelled. The heart like a lotus blossoms and eternal peace is procured, when man's light merges with the supreme light.
3rd (**126**/1/418)

In the mansion are treasures brimful with jewels. Through the Guru, man obtains the treasures of the infinite name. The pious trader always purchases the goods of the name and always earns a profit.
3rd (**126**/1/418)

Under the Guru's guidance, he who searches this cave, finds the enemy of ego, the pure name, abiding within his mind.
3rd (**127**/1/419)

When the perfect true Guru preached to me his gospel, I discovered the priceless wealth of

God's name in my own home. By the Guru's grace the darkness of ignorance is dispelled and with the divine light in my mind, I have recognised my own self.
3rd (**128-129**/1/426)

Within the mind is the unseen Lord, but he cannot be seen. Taking the jewel of the name, he has kept it concealed within. The unapproachable and inapprehensible Lord is the highest of all. By the Guru's instruction he is known.
3rd (**130**/1/431)

They who meditate on the master are not thrown into hell. Even the hot wind touches them not, within whose mind the Lord has come and acquired an abode.
3rd (**132**/1/438)

If the true Guru be mightily pleased, man finds the treasure of the jewel within him. Without the Guru, no one has found the treasure. The false and the blind have perished in ceaseless wanderings.
Ist (**141**/1/467)

Nanak, through the true *Gurbani*, the one in whose mind the truth abides gets absorbed in God's name.
Ist (**141**/1/469)

Looking around in four directions, I searched my inner self. There I saw the invisible true Lord, the creator. I strayed in the wilderness. The Guru has shown me the way. Hail to the true Sat-Guru, through whom I have remembered the true Lord. The Guru has lighted the lamp and within my home, I have found the emerald.
Ist (**149**/1/497-8)

O my mind, within thee is the treasure, search not for the thing without. O my soul, the Lord and master, the helper is within thee. Be holy and see him with thine eyes.
3rd (**569**/4/1870)

Searching abroad, thou shalt suffer much pain. The nectar is in thy heart at home.
Ist (**598**/4/1965)

Whatever is seen, that is the Lord himself. Creating himself the Lord installs the soul in the body.
Ist (**931**/6/3037)

What can man say of the Lord, whom he cannot see? I am a sacrifice unto my Guru, who has shown me my master within my mind.
Ist (**937**/6/3061)

By the Guru's grace the true Lord abides in man's mind and he then strikes a true bargain.
Everything is within the home. The very fortunate ones alone obtain it.
Ist (**955**/6/3131)

I wandered from village to village and through all the cities, but through the Lord's slaves, I found God in my own mind.
4th (**983**/6/3221)

The jewel of the name within stills the mind and being attached to truth the mind does not suffer separation.
Ist (992/6/3250)

He who always serves his Lord day and night ends doubt and the name abides in his mind.
Ist (992/6/3252)

By meeting with God I have become one with him and I am blessed with supreme pleasure and peace, says Nanak.
5th (999/6/3274)

I have given up searching abroad. The Guru has shown my Lord within my home.
5th (1002/6/3282)

My desire is stilled. The Lord of inexhaustible treasure has entered my mind and now I feel no want.
5th (1002/6/3283)

If, through the Guru's instruction, man enshrines in his mind, God, the life of the world, he will save his entire lineage.
Ist (1009/6/3305)

The wealth of the Lord's name gives immortality. The Guru enshrines it in the mind and heart.
Ist(1012/6/3315)

If through the Guru's pleasure the name abides in man's mind, then day and night, he remains absorbed in the Lord's love.
Ist (1015/6/3329)

The Guru has shown such a miracle that within my own mind, I now enjoy my Lord God, says Nanak.
5th (1018/6/3338)

Utter the truth and realise the Lord is within. He is not far off. See him with a glance ... Within the body abides the Lord's name.
Ist (1026/6/3364)

Within the village of the body is the castle of the mind. Within the city of the tenth gate is the abode of the true Lord.
Ist (1033/6/3388)

Within the fortress is the cave of the tenth gate, the Lord's home. By his order, the Lord has established nine apertures to the house of the body ... The incomparable and infinite Lord abides in the tenth gate. The invisible God reveals his own self. Within the body of air, water and fire dwells the one Lord. He himself stages the play and the drama.
Ist (1033/6/3389)

Binding together air, water and fire, he has created the fortress of the body. To it the creator has fixed the nine doors. In the tenth gate is the abode of the indiscernable, infinite Lord.
Ist (1036/6/3400)

The creator Lord has fixed nine doors to the township of the body. Within the tenth gate abides the detached and unequalled Lord.

The inscrutable Lord himself makes one realise the Lord. The inscrutable Lord makes one realise himself ... Within the mansion abides the Lord and he rids man of comings and goings.
Ist (1039/6/3413)

He who realises the Lord is purged of the filth of sins. The immaculate name comes and abides within his mind.
3rd (1044/6/3429)

By showering his benedictions on man, he himself abides in man's mind. Such is the command of my master.
3rd (1046/6/3437)

Searching his body, by the Guru's grace, man finds the bounteous Lord, the life of the world. The Lord delivers the body fortress seized by sins, and the mortal ever keeps the Lord enshrined within his mind.
3rd (1051/6/3455)

In the body fortress are many shops and bazaars. Therein is the name of the exceedingly infinite Lord.
3rd (1053/6/3459)

Within the filthy body and mind is the light of the infinite Lord. He who reflects over the Guru's gospel understands this.
3rd (1053/6/3459)

Unfathomable and unknowable is the Lord. He cannot be evaluated.

By the Guru's grace, he is enshrined in the mind.
3rd (1053/6/3462)

One ought to search for him within and praise the Lord. Why should he run without? He who recognises himself understands all the virtues. By the Guru's instruction, he repeats the Lord's name.
3rd (1056/6/3473)

The mortal man reads the Vedas and through reading them enters into controversies. Within his mind is the Lord, but he does not realise his name.
3rd (1058/6/3477)

The follower of the Guru searches his mind and utters what he sees there. He ever embodies love for the true name.
3rd (1059/6/3480)

When he so wills, he makes man meet the true Guru. When it pleases him, then he enshrines his name within man's mind.
3rd (1059/6/3481)

The body is the Lord's mansion. God himself embellishes it. Within that abides the Lord, the enemy of ego.
3rd (1059/6/3483)

Within our home is the true Lord. Rare is the one, who realises this by the Guru's grace.
3rd (1060/6/3484)

Serving the true Guru man obtains poise and pleasure, and the Lord of the universe comes to abide in his mind.
3rd (**1062**/6/3494)

He has put everything within this body ... Reflecting on the name, the body becomes like gold. There God abides, who has no limits or bounds.
3rd (**1064**/6/3500)

The body becomes immaculate through the Guru's word. Within abides the true Lord, the ocean of virtues.
3rd (**1065**/6/3502)

He alone meditates on the Lord, whom the Lord himself causes to meditate. Through the Guru's word the Lord comes to abide in the mortal's mind.
3rd (**1065**/6/3502)

It is within the body that man loses and within the body that he gains.
3rd (**1066**/6/3506)

Within the body is the commodity of the name. Its worth cannot be found. Unto the lover of the Guru he grants glory.
3rd (**1066**/6/3507)

The reverend Lord is contained amongst all. By the Guru's grace he is obtained.
3rd (**1066**/6/3507)

They who search their body, reflect on the name, discard the poisonous potion of worldly love and dispel their doubts.
3rd (**1068**/6/3514)

He, who instinctively utters the Lord's praises day and night, will find his light merges in the supreme light.
3rd (**1068**/6/3514)

Within the minds of all abides the true Lord. By the Guru's grace, man merges in the Lord.
4th (**1069**/6/3515)

Reflecting on the Guru's word, the Lord's name has secured an abode within my mind.
4th (**1087**/6/3575)

If the peace giving Lord abides in man's mind here, then he becomes his succour in the end.
4th (**1087**/6/3577)

If the true Sat-Guru abides within my mind, I see my Lord, the friend, in that very place. By singing the praises of the true name, the soul is satiated, O Nanak.
Ist (**1087**/6/3577)

Nanak has been transported by obtaining within his mind thy name, O spouse.
5th (**1098**/6/3614)

The master is within my mind. His name I utter and repeat with my mouth.
5th (**1098**/6/3616)

Nanak, I have obtained deep vision and peace and with the Guru's word my soul is consoled.
Ist (**1107**/7/3646)

O Lord, I know thee not afar, I believe thee to be within me and realise thy presence.
I (**1108**/7/3648)

God, the life of the world, permeates my mind and body. Through the Guru's word I enjoy his love.
Ist (**1109**/7/3652)

Having the Guru's vision, spiritual ignorance is dispelled and the light becomes manifest in the mind.
The pain of birth and death is stilled in an instant and the imperishable Lord God is obtained.
4th (**1116**/7/3675)

By searching my mind and body, I have obtained the Lord in my own home.
3rd (**1130**/7/3717)

The Guru has shown me the inaccessible, inapprehensible and carefree Lord. Searching within the township of the body, I have discovered my God.
4th (**1134**/7/3732)

My father has become manifest within my mind. Father and son have met together in partnership.
5th (**1141**/7/3756)

The mortal who serves the Lord, becomes pure and through the

Guru's instruction banishes his self-conceit from within himself. The venerable Lord himself comes to abide in his mind and he ever remains merged in tranquillity, peace and praise.
3rd (**1173**/7/3866)

Standing within my mind, the Lord has made me meditate on his feet.
5th (**1193**/7/3933)

Within thee abides thy Lord and by the Guru's grace, he is seen to be always present.
3rd (**1283-4**/7/4235)

God comes and abides in the minds of those who are thus predestined.
4th (**1313-4**/8/4335)

In the hamlet or township of the body abides the Lord, and through the counsel of the Guru, the Lord God becomes manifest. In the pool of the body, God's name has become manifest and within my home palace, I have obtained my Lord God.
4th (**1336**/8/4409)

God dwells in the abode and palace of the body and by the Guru's grace, I dwell upon the meditation of him and his praise.
4th (**1336**/8/4410)

Uniting the five elements together, the Lord has given them a false gilding. When it pleases him, he sets the vessel alright.

Then in it supreme light shines
and the celestial strains resound.
Ist (**1411/8/4664**)

6. Salvation through the society of saints

Anyone who joins the society of saints or the congregation of the righteous will cross over the world ocean and cut the noose of death. The Guru gives the prize of salvation to the society of saints. The society of saints, like the Guru, can only be found by the greatest good luck, if you are so destined. The original for "the society of saints" is "Gur Sant Sabha", which the translator renders "the Guru saint".

The Guru gives the wealth of salvation; in the society of saints the elysian cow is obtained.
Ist (**18/1/57**)

In the society of saints the mortal becomes pure and the noose of death is cut.
5th (**44/1/150**)

By meeting the society of saints and acting upon the Guru's instructions, the mortal is saved ... Through the society of saints, the beloved Lord, the pardoner, abides in one's mind.
5th (**49/1/164**)

The Lord is obtained in the society of saints, when the Guru, the uniter, unites man thereby.
Ist (**56-7/1/192**)

By joining the congregation of the saints, I have found God, my

friend. I am devoted to the true Guru.
4th (**96**/1/321)

In the society of saints thou shalt be saved in a moment. Thy mind shall be purged clean of sins and thy comings and goings shall cease.
5th (**103**/1/342)

He who comes from home and joins the society of the saints, with hearty aspiration, gets rid of birth and death.
5th (**104**/1/344)

In the congregation of the righteous thou shalt cross the world ocean and cut the noose of death.
5th (**108**/1/357)

The true Lord blends with himself those, who join the congregation of the saints and sing his true praises.
3rd (**120**/1/397)

The saints, who render man assistance, have mercifully united me with the all-pervading Lord.
5th (**136**/1/450)

Show mercy, O Lord God, the searcher of hearts, that through the society of saints, I may obtain thee.
5th (**383**/3/1273)

In the society of pious persons all sins are eradicated.
4th (**652**/4/2140)

Associating with the pious, sing the Lord's praises. Thus shalt thou be rid of the pain of millions of births.
5th (**720**/4/2352)

Without enmity are the saints of the supreme Lord. Whoever worships their feet is emancipated.
5th (**1145**/7/3769)

By associating with the Guru saint, miseries and maladies are ended. Servant Nanak has easily met his God, the spouse.
(Note: The original word is 'Gur Sant Sabha'. "The saints' congregation" is being spoken of as "the Guru saint" by the translator.)
Ist (**1170**/7/3854)

They who associate with the saints' society have all their sins washed away and they are emancipated. Seeing them God becomes merciful and they cross the dreadful world ocean.
5th (**1235**/7/4071)

Through the greatest good fortune, I have attained to the holy congregation of the saints and by association with the saints, I am ferried across the ocean.
4th (**1264**/7/4171)

I have come to the saints to save myself. Seeing a vision of them, I am rendered spotless and they have implanted the Lord God's name within me.
5th (**1299**/8/4288)

Since the time, I have attained to the society of saints, I have altogether forgotten to be jealous of others.
No one now is my enemy, nor is anyone a stranger to me and I am the friend of all.
Whatever the Lord does, that I deem to be good. This sublime wisdom I have obtained from the saints.
5th (**1299**/8/4288-9)

By associating with the society of the saints, the noose of death has been cut and one merges with his Lord, O Nanak.
5th (**1300**/8/4290)

By contemplating the Lord in the society of the saints man's comings and goings are ended and his sufferings are effaced as well.
5th (**1300**/8/4291)

Whoever bathes in the dust of the saints' feet, he washes away the sins of myriads of births.
5th (**1300**/8/4292)

Nanak, the beggar asks for the Lord God's name and rests his forehead on the feet of his Lord.
5th (**1301**/8/4295)

By great good fortune, one is blessed with the saints' society and the perfect word of the great true Guru.
4th (**1317-8**/8/4348-9)

B. Permanency of salvation

Once merged with God man is never separated from him again. In this respect salvation is permanent, as man becomes God himself by merging with God; man's light merges into the supreme light.

Once merged with God, man is never separated from him again and his light merges into the supreme light.
3rd (**1247**/7/4115)

They who are united with God are never separated again. The creator has united them with himself.
3rd (**1249**/7/4122)

Whoever meets with the primal Lord is never separated again.
3rd (**1262**/7/4163)

C. Exclusive claims for peace and salvation by the Gurus

The Gurus claim the following: that the Guru is the sole custodian of salvation. That salvation cannot be found anywhere without the Guru. That salvation can only be found through the name, by the help of the Guru. That God can only be found within your mind, not outside.

The true merchandise is in only one shop. It is obtained from the perfect Guru.
2nd (**146**/1/486)

The dispenser of peace is the one Lord alone. From no other can peace be procured.
3rd (**1132**/7/3725)

Without the Guru, one cannot be emancipated anywhere in the three worlds.
Ist (**1171**/7/3860)

Nanak, there is but one nectar-giving name. There is no other nectar.
2nd (**1238**/7/4082)

D. The grace of God in the Granth

How can a sinner recognise himself and the Guru, in order to be united with God the creator? Through God's order of things (Hukam), God's truth is revealed, but only a few can perceive that, because of the ill effects of past Karma. Only people who have enough merit from their previous births are able to recognise the Guru. This is called the pre-requisite perception[1]. God causes them to meet the Guru, who then helps them meet with God through the Nam (name).

But sinners need God's pre-requisite grace or divine gift of perception through his favourable glance, called Nadar, *in order to meet the name-giving Guru, which God in his mercy grants to some and not to the rest. God through his grace then causes the person to meet the Guru and through the Guru unites him with himself.*

A person who bows down to God's order in creation or his Bhana or Raza (will) cannot question the creator as to why he has granted his favour to some and left out others. It is in fact a mystery of God according to the Gurus. This bestowal of grace upon the sinner is a prerequisite gift of perception

---

[1]   Guru Nanak and the Sikh Religion, by W.H. McLeod, p. 204

or a means to salvtion and not salvation itself. It only helps to recognise the Guru and meditate upon the name. Man still needs to earn the Guru's grace through his service to the Guru and has to work hard under the discipline of the Guru through meditation on the Nam, in order to meet with God in the mansion of his mind, at the Dasham-Dwar *(tenth gate). His light then merges with the supreme light. Some other words have also been used for grace such as* Kirpa, Karam, Daya, Mehar, Tarab *and* Bakhshish *etc.*

There are a great many references in the Granth to back this doctrine of which the following are a small selection.

By good actions the physical robe (body) is obtained and by the Lord's benediction the gate of salvation.
1st (**2**/1/3)

By God's grace, his name is meditated upon. Without his favour it cannot be obtained.
3rd (**35**/1/120)

If the Lord shows his mercy, he merges man with himself.
3rd (**35-6**/1/121)

If God's grace rests upon us, it is then that we obtain the name. Of ourselves we cannot find it.
*I*st (**61**/1/207)

Through God's grace truth is attained to. No one can efface the primordial gift.
*I*st (**62**/1/212)

The Guru firmly installs God's name with love, but without his grace, the name cannot be attained to.
3rd (**65**/1/223)

By the Guru's grace the Lord is obtained and it is through good luck that the Guru is met.
3rd (**65**/1/223)

Nanak, greatness is in the name of God. By the Lord's power the name is attained to.
3rd (**66**/1/226)

The followers of the Guru serve the true Lord, who comes and takes abode in their heart.
They ever remain imbued with the love of the true being, who by showering on them his benediction unites them with himself.
3rd (**69**/1/235)

By the casting of his merciful glance, God unites man with himself.
*I*st (**72**/1/244)

If the Lord casts his merciful glance, he unites man with himself.
*I*st (**72**/1/246)

By showering his mercy on me, he has blended me with himself.
*I*st (**72**/1/247)

They whom the Lord mercifully unites with the Guru, repeat the name of Lord God.
4th (**77**/1/260)

Those with whom the Lord, the treasure of excellence, is mightily pleased obtain the Guru, O servant Nanak!
4th (**82-3**/1/278)

What is a swan and what is a crane? The Lord may show mercy to any he likes. He who is pleasing to the Lord is changed by him, as if from a crow into a swan, O Nanak!
Ist (**91**/1/305)

O venerable God! show mercy and cause me to meet the Guru. From him slave Nanak shall gather the wealth of God's name, in his lap.
4th (**98**/1/315)

By thy grace, I understand thee. Thou art my covering and thou art my honour.
5th (**103**/1/343)

By the Lord's grace the true Guru is met. Then alone does man apply his attention to God's service and fix his mind on his name.
3rd (**110**/1/363)

The extent of the inaccessible and incomprehensible Lord cannot be known.
Showing thy mercy, thou blendest the mortal with thyself.
3rd (**130**/1/430)

From the blind well, thou hast dragged me out onto the dry shore. By thy mercy, thou hast beheld thy servants with gracious glances.
3rd (**132**/1/436)

The Lord bestows this light on him on whom he casts his merciful glance. Through the Guru he (such a man) receives the jewel of the name, O Nanak.
3rd (**145**/1/483)

Unto me the meritless ursurper, the Lord has become merciful.
5th (**1142**/7/3757)

The devoteee, whom the Lord himself in his mercy saves, utters and repeats the Lord's name.
5th (**1147**/7/3777)

The entire spiritual darkness of the one, whom the saviour saves in his mercy, is dispelled.
5th (**1148**/7/3780)

When God shows mercy, man is rid of his ego. He then obtains honour in the true court.
3rd (**1173**/7/3864)

God, of himself does all. Of himself man cannot do a thing. When the Lord wills, he merges man with himself.
3rd (**1175**/7/3873)

Showing his mercy, the Lord has come to his slave.
5th (**1237**/7/4076)

He alone is emancipated, on whom God bestows his grace.
3rd (**1261**/7/4161)

The Lord is the purifier of sinners, the lover of his devotees and the ocean of mercy.
5th (**1278**/7/4215)

Whosoever receives God's grace, he alone knows the virtuous way of life.
1st (**1330**/8/4390)

My unfathomable and compassionate Lord and master, has shown me mercy and I now utter his name with my mouth.
4th (**1336**/8/4409)

The Lord of the world has become merciful and my sufferings and sins have been wiped away in a moment.
5th (**1338**/8/4417)

E. What is the *Nam* (the name of God)?

The Nam or the name of God is not an abstract word but the manifestation of God himself that comes to stay in the mind of a person through the Guru. It can also be one of the thousands of names of God, used in order to call upon him through meditation, when it pertains to a particular name of God either qualitative or unqualitative.

Unfathomable, unweighable and supremely priceless is this treasure of the name.[2] The name is my immovable master. The supreme[3] Guru's word is the Lord's name and this name, I enshrine in my mind.
2nd (**1239**/7/4083)

Note: The exclusiveness of the name

Without the Lord's name, no one obtains salvation and all are drowned but without water.
Ist (**1127**/7/3704)

In the dark age, one is emancipated only through the name.
5th (**1138**/7/3744)

Without the name, no one obtains emancipation.
3rd (**1175**/7/3872)

Glorious is the Lord's praise and the Lord's name. It is the sublime deed in the dark age.
4th (**1314**/8/4336)

---

[2] In the original there is no word for name. Perhaps the translator has ascribed divine attributes to the name on the basis of the next line.

[3] There is no word for supreme Guru in the original. It is only *Gurmukhi-Bani* (Guru's word).

F. Who gives the *Nam*?

1. Guru gives the *Nam*

The name of God comes and abides in the mind of him who is under the Guru's instruction, who while alive remains dead.
3rd (**33**/1/114)

The Guru firmly installs God's name with love, but without his grace, the name cannot be attained to.
3rd (**65**/1/223)

Through the Guru man easily obtains the wealth of God's name.
3rd (**69**/1/228)

When the Guru is mightily pleased, the true name is obtained, O Nanak.
3rd (**71**/1/241)

Everyone longs for thy name. Without the true Guru thou art not found.
Ist (**71-2**/1/242)

God is mine and I am a slave of his, O Nanak! The Guru has given me the true name.
5th (**100-1**/1/335)

True is the Lord and true his name. By the Guru's grace, I please him in my mind.
3rd (**110**/1/364)

The true Guru, the giver, is met when God causes man to meet him. By perfect destiny God's name is enshrined in man's mind.
3rd (**115**/1/381)

Through the Guru man obtains those treasures of the infinite name.
3rd (**126**/1/418)

Under the Guru's guidance he who searches this cave, finds the pure name of the enemy of ego abiding in his mind.
3rd (**127**/1/419)

The wealth of God's name gives immortality. The Guru enshrines it in the mind and the heart
Ist (**1012**/6/3315)

By the Guru's grace, the immaculate Lord's name is obtained and the unendurable load of sins is removed.
Ist (**1013**/6/3322)

By the Guru's grace, one obtains the wealth of the name.
4th (**1069**/6/3517)

The true Guru is the banker who possesses the treasure of the name. This gem of the Lord's name is obtained from him.
5th (**1078**/6/3566)

The Lord's name which is the wealth and support of all, is obtained in the mind by the Guru's grace.
Ist (**1127**/7/3704)

But without the Lord's name, he does not obtain emancipation and the redeeming name, which one gains by the Guru's grace.
1st (**1127/7/3704**)

By the Guru's grace, I meditate on the name of God.
5th (**1148/7/3778**)

When the Guru is merciful, man contemplates his God and en-shrines the Lord and the Lord's name within his mind.
4th (**1314/8/4336**)

The treasure of bliss is the name of the Lord. It is by the Guru's grace that one attains it.
4th (**1316/8/4344**)

By grasping the feet of the saint, I have attained the nectar of the name, says Nanak.
5th (**1322/8/4363**)

2. God gives the *Nam*

If God shows his mercy, then man comes to profess love for the name.
3rd (**34**/1/116)

God's name alone is the ambrosial fruit; he himself gives it.
3rd (**66**/1/224)

The Lord himself summons and bestows his name.
3rd (**117-8**/1/389)

Nanak, the Lord's name abides within his mind. He, unto whom the Lord donates his name, attains to it.
3rd (**118**/1/389)

When it pleases him, then the Lord merges the mortal with himself.
3rd (**128**/1/424)

The Lord merges with himself those who ever keep in view the Guru's instructions.
3rd (**129-130**/1/429)

When he so wills, he makes man meet the true Guru. When it pleases him, then he enshrines his name within man's mind.
3rd (**1059**/6/3483)

By reflecting on the Guru's word, the Lord's name has secured an abode within my mind.
4th (**1087**/6/3575)

He alone receives the name, to whom the Lord gives it.
5th (**1148**/7/3781)

God's name abides only within the mind of the one whom the Lord blesses with this gift.
4th (**1298**/8/4285)

G. Who can receive the *Nam*?

1. One who has such a destiny

He alone is blessed with the name, on whose forehead it (destiny) is so writ.
5th (**1304**/8/4305)

They alone meditate on God's name, on whose forehead it is so written by God.
4th (**1316**/8/4344)

Through perfect good fortune (destiny), the Guru is obtained.
3rd (**115**/1/380)

2. One who serves the Guru

By performing service to the Guru, the name is gained and one remains absorbed in the true Lord.
3rd (**34**/1/114)

I submit to the will of the true Guru and have expelled self-conceit from within me. This is the service and meditation of the Lord, by which the name comes and dwells in my mind.
3rd (**34**/1/117)

This true soul is dyed in the true name and remains absorbed in the true Lord. In speech, sight and utterance this soul remains permeated by the name.
3rd (**35**/1/119)

Without serving the Guru, peace is not produced. Through perfect good fortune, the Guru is obtained.
3rd (**115**/1/380)

From the Guru's service God's name is obtained. Without the true Guru no one can receive the Lord's name.
3rd (**116**/1/383)

Without serving the true Guru, no one is emancipated; let anyone enquire from the divines and con-templatives.
3rd (**1052**/6/3491)

If man serves the true Guru, then he is emancipated and overcomes the five demons.
3rd (**1068**/6/3513)

By the Guru's grace, they utter and repeat God's name.
4th (**1069**/6/3518)

H. How the Guru is found

The Guru is obtained by perfect destiny

The true Guru, the bestower, has implanted God's name in my heart. By the greatest good luck I have obtained a sight of the Guru.
4th (**96**/1/320)

Through perfect good fortune the Guru is obtained.
3rd (**115**/1/380)

The true Guru, the giver, is met when God causes man to meet him. By perfect destiny God's name is enshrined in man's mind.
3rd (**115**/1/381)

By perfect good destiny, they attain to the true Guru, who unites them through the name in union with the Lord.
3rd (**122**/1/405)

In the true Guru's hand is the key, no one else can open the door. By perfect good luck the Guru is met.
3rd (**124**/1/412)

Those who are so predestined, meet with their Guru.
3rd (**1415**/8/4678)

7

GURUSHIP

Introduction

1. **God as Guru**

2. **The Word as Guru**

3. **The personal Guru**

4. **Limitations of the personal Gurus**

5. **Mysterious sayings of the Gurus**

6. **Guidelines for following the Guru**

Introduction

The concept of guruship and discipleship is basic to the Sikh faith. The very word *"Sikh"* means a disciple or a learner, who goes on following the Guru in order to learn the vital truth which the Guru conveys. However, it is not always clear in the Granth, who the Guru really is. Principal Teja Singh gives this definition, as quoted by Mcleod in his book *Guru Nanak and the Sikh Faith,* "Guru is a particular personality, a creative and perfect personality who stands as guide and exemplar. This personality inhabited the ten personal Gurus and with the death of Guru Govind Singh merged in the scriptures and in the community." (p. 197)

This definition makes it clear that primarily *God himself is the Guru.* He is called *Sat-Guru* and *Waheguru* (praise to the God Guru). Guru Arjan Dev makes this clear when he says that, "The true Guru is *Niranjan* (the formless one); do not believe that he is in the form of a man." This concept also helps us to understand who Guru Nanak's Guru was, as he did not have a human Guru. It however poses a dilemma, when this God Guru helps a devotee to meet God the creator through the *Nam* and the creator Lord comes to stay in the mind, in the place called the tenth gate. Can we say in the words of the Gurus that God himself helps people to meet himself?

Secondly, the fact that God is the Guru requires the provision of a *personal human Guru,* who acts as the agent of the Niranjan Guru, as the conveyor and communicator of his truth to mankind. He is nothing more than an agent of the supreme Guru, the creator himself. Therefore, we see a separate place given for the personal human Guru, as the communicator of divine truth to mankind in the Granth.

Thirdly, we see the work of the unseen, invisible agent of God, which Mcleod calls the *inner voice* or God's light as Guru, permeating the human mind and body. To call this inner voice a Guru is questionable, but it is vital and useful to human personality, keeping the hunger for God alive and giving man a sense of right and wrong. It does not necessarily guide all persons to God or help them recognise God as Guru easily. Thousands of prayers by the Gurus themselves crying out to God to reveal himself even for a moment demonstrate this. However, we can safely agree with Mcleod when he says: "A strict definition requires us to identify the Guru, not with God himself, but with the voice of God, with the means whereby God imparts truth to man."

Fourthly, *the word as Guru*. When asked, "Who is your Guru?", Guru Nanak replied:

"The word is the Guru and mind (which is focused on it) continually is the disciple. By dwelling on the ineffable one, on him the eternal Guru-Gopal, I remain detached. It is only through the word that I dwell on him and so through the Guru the fire of *Haumai* is extinguished."
Ist (**943**/6/3081-2)

1. God as Guru

With love adore the Lord incarnate Guru in body and mind. The true Guru is the bestower of life and lends support to all.
5th (**52**/1/176)

The Guru is omnipotent and the Guru is infinite. It is through the greatest good luck that a view of him is obtained.
Imperceptible and immaculate is the Guru. No one else is as great as the Guru.
The Guru is the creator and the Guru is the doer. It is through the Guru that true glory is obtained.
Nothing is beyond (the jurisdiction of) the Guru.
Whatever the Guru desires comes to pass.
The Guru is the place of pilgrimage, the Guru is the elysian (*kalpa*) tree and the Guru is the fulfiller of desire.
The Guru is the giver and grants God's name, wherewith the entire world is saved.
The Guru is patient (enough) to do everything and the Guru is himself the formless Lord. The Guru is high, unfathomable and limitless.
5th (**52**/1/177)

Whilst drawing breath and taking food, I forget not the Guru, who by himself possesses an accredited personality. None is seen to be as great as the Guru, so reflect on him, throughout the eight watches of the day. The

Guru and God are one and the divine Guru is contained amongst all.
5th (**53**/1/179)

All are apt to commit error. The Guru and the creator alone are infallible.
Ist (**61**/1/207)

Whosoever is come, he shall go, only the sublime Guru and the creator are eternal.
Ist (**63**/1/216)

Know no difference between the exalted Sat-Guru and the Lord, by meeting whom the Lord's devotional service is endeared to man.
4th (**77**/1/260)

The true Guru is all-powerful. If I remember him within my mind, it is then that all my sorrows depart.
5th (**98-9**/1/329)

They who contemplate God, the incarnate, perfect Guru, are judged as true and genuine in his court.
5th (**136**/1/451)

The Guru is the giver, the Guru is the house of ice and the Guru is the lamp (light) of the three worlds. The Guru possesses eternal wealth, O Nanak, and by putting the hearts' faith in him peace is obtained.
Ist (**137**/1/455)

Worship thou the Guru-God and dedicate this soul of thine to him. He is the very image of the immortal one.
5th (**614**/4/2017)

The Lord (*Guru Govinda*) is my physician.
5th(**618**/4/2028)

The Lord himself is the Guru, the disciple and the performer of wondrous frolics.
4th (**669**/4/2195)

The Guru is the master, the Guru is the Lord and the Guru is the pervading Lord.
The Guru is compassionate, the Guru is omnipotent and the Guru is the saviour of sinners.
The Guru is the ship to cross over the dangerous, formidable and unfathomable world ocean.
5th (**710**/4/2322)

The supreme Lord master, under whose sway are all sentient beings, is himself the true Guru.
5th (**825**/5/2686)

By great good luck, I have met the perfect wise and omniscient Guru, the inner knower.
5th (**825**/5/2687)

Hide thou my faults, O my Guru-God. I, a sinner, have sought the refuge of thy feet.
5th (**828**/5/2694)

Enshrine thou the Guru's feet in thy mind. Ever make thou obeis-

ance unto the Guru, thy supreme Lord.
5th (864/5/2812)

The Guru is the creator and the Guru is potent to do everything. The Guru-God is and also shall be.
5th (864/5/2813)

I worship only my Guru. My Guru is himself the Lord. My Guru is the transcendent Lord and my Guru is the auspicious master.
5th (864/5/2814)

Make thou obeisance unto thy perfect Guru-God ... He is the inner knower, the creator Lord. The Guru is the master of the universe and the cherisher of the world. He destroys the arrogant villains.
5th (869/5/2830)

When the mind is wholly held, then the mortal deems Guru and God as one and the same.
5th (887/6/2889)

My Guru-God is the giver of peace. He plants the supreme Lord's name in me and shall be my helper in the end.
5th (915/6/2983)

The Lord himself is the exalted Guru. He blesses man with the nectar name and makes him quaff his nectar.
Ist (930/6/3032)

Within the Guru, the creator has placed his own self. By the Guru's grace countless millions are saved .... The Guru himself is the immaculate, inscrutable and infinite Lord.
Ist (1024/6/3357)

He himself is the true Guru, himself the attendant and of himself he creates the world.
Ist (1025/6/3362)

My Lord is inaccessible, incomprehensible, unfathomable and detached. The limit of the Guru-God cannot be found.
Ist (1027/6/3369)

O my Guru-God, I have entered thy sanctuary. Thou thyself art the omnipotent and compassionate Lord, the enemy of ego.
Ist (1031/6/3381)

The Guru is the cherisher of the world and the Guru is the master of the universe. The Guru is the compassionate and ever forgiving. ... Remembering the Guru all sins are effaced and remembering the Guru, one is not entangled in death's noose.
5th (1074/6/3534)

God's slave is like unto the Lord. Due to his human body deem him not distinct from the Lord.
5th (1076/6/3538)

The true personality of the true Guru is the embodiment of the transcendent Lord; by meeting him one is ferried across.
5th (1078/6/3545)

He, the true Guru, is himself the inapprehensible transcendent Lord. He alone whom the Guru yokes to his service and on whose forehead good fortune is recorded is said to be his slave.
5th (**1078**/6/3545-6)

The true Guru is the most excellent supreme Lord, contemplating whom the soul is cooled.
5th (**1078**/6/3546)

The Guru is the supreme Lord and the Guru is the master of the universe. The Guru is the creator and the Guru is the ever forgiving Lord.
5th (**1080**/6/3553-4)

The great Guru, the true Guru, is himself the Lord. Consult thou the *Smritis*. They too establish this truth. The *Smritis* and *Shashtras* all prove that the Guru is the em-bodiment of God.
4th (**1117**/7/3678)

The Guru is God and unfathomable and inscrutable is the Guru. Through the Guru's service the knowledge of the three worlds is acquired. The beneficent Guru of himself has given me the gift and I have obtained the invisible and mysterious Lord.
Ist (**1125**/7/3703)

O, my benevolent, omnipotent, divine and beneficent true Guru, I am a sinner and thou art my pardoner.
5th (**1141**/7/3756)

I make obeisance unto my true Guru, the transcendent Lord.
5th (**1141**/7/3757)

My true Guru is the giver of all. The true Guru is my creator Lord.
5th (**1142**/7/3758)

My true Guru slays and revives the mortal.
5th (**1142**/7/3758)

Between the transcendent Lord and the Guru, there is no difference.
5th (**1142**/7/3758-9)

O, my soul, meditate thou on thy Guru-God.
5th (**1149**/7/3782)

My Lord Guru has heard my prayer.
5th (**1152**/7/3794)

My powerful Guru-God is the greatest of all.
5th (**1152**/7/3794)

Of peerless beauty is my supreme Lord and master. The accredited personality of the Guru is the embodiment of that Lord.
5th (**1152**/7/3795)

He who shows the Lord's abode within man's mind, he alone is the omnipotent and omniscient, true Guru.
Ist (**1290-1**/7/4261)

The true Guru has become merciful unto me, the meek one, and he

has shown me the way and the path of God.
4th (**1311/8/4327**)

Nanak, the Guru is the embodiment of the Lord God, by meeting whom, one is blessed with God's name.
4th (**1313/8/4332**)

The Guru is my unfathomable Lord and I am his child; in his mercy, the Guru sustains me.
4th (**1335/8/4407**)

My Guru is all powerful and ever merciful.
5th (**1341/8/4424**)

My Guru-God has saved me from them.
5th (**1347/8/4446**)

When man meets with the true Guru, then alone does he attain unto the perfect Lord and his tongue enjoys the elixir of the Guru's name.
4th (**1318/8/4351**)

2. The Word as Guru

Note: Manmohan Singh has translated Shabad (word) as Lord (Guru). The original refers to Shabad (word) as Guru. We want to retain the word Shabad, and prefer to translate it as Word, in order to clarify the concept of Word as Guru.

The *Word* is my Guru, on which, I, his disciple, greatly love to meditate.
Uttering the discourse of the ineffable Lord, I remain detached.
Nanak, through all the ages, God, the cherisher of the world, is my Guru.
Such is the unique Word (*shabad*), by meditating on whose divine discourse, man crosses the terrible ocean. Thus does the Guru word quench his fire of self-conceit.
1st (**943/6/3082**)

The true Guru is the Word and the Word is the true Guru. The holy Word shows the way to emancipation.
4th (**1309/8/4322**)

Note: also that Shabad is often interchanged with Nam (name), as in the following passages:

The world is hard for the wayward fool. Practising the Name (*shabad*), iron is chewed with waxen teeth.
1st (**943/6/3083**)

Enshrining the true Name (*shabad*) in his mind and cooling and dyeing his body and soul with the love of the Lord, man abides in the home and mansion of snow.
Ist (**943**/6/3083)

Uttering God's Name (*shabad*), the mind moon is infinitely illumined.
When the sun abides in the moon's house, it blazes and the darkness is dispelled.
Ist (**943**/6/3084)

3. The personal Guru

The Guru in human form is also very important, such as the ten Gurus. The human Guru plays an important role in explaining the divine truths to seekers or disciples. This personal Guru when united to God through merger becomes God himself, thereby ending transmigration and remaining in God as God himself forever.

Receiving the Guru's instruction, he meditates on the Lord's name and by good fortune embracing the Lord's love, he himself becomes the Lord.
4th (**576**/4/1892)

Nanak knows this truth, that the Lord is not different from his saint.
5th (**578**/4/1898)

As water mixing with water, blends therewith, so merges the saints' light with supreme light.
5th (**578**/4/1899)

The light of the pure Lord, the essence of everything, pervades all. I am he and there is no difference.
Ist (**599**/4/1968)

No one can undo the Guru's order. Nanak is the Guru and Nanak himself is the Lord.
5th (**865**/5/2815)

God's slave, he is like unto the Lord. Due to his human body deem him not distinct from the Lord.
5th (**1076/6/3538**)

Meeting with the philosopher's stone, they themselves are transmuted into the philosopher's stone and become the comrades of the divine Guru.
Ist (**1172/7/3860**)

The perfect Guru has blessed me with all the fruits and the Guru has emancipated me, O Nanak.
5th (**1218/7/4013**)

Says Nanak, the Guru has broken my bonds and has united me with God, from whom I was separated.
5th (**1219/7/4015**)

Says Nanak, God's slave is himself the Lord God, hence he does not need to come, nor to go.
5th (**1302/8/4297**)

God, the Lord God, has placed his own self in his slave. As such, his slave and the Lord God are one and the same, O Nanak.
4th (**1336-7/8/4411**)

4. Limitations of the personal Gurus

The Gurus face certain limitations, like any other human beings, before their merger with God. They face temptations, doubt, the pain of being without God and their frustration about the political situation of their times. The violent onslaughts by the Mughais on the Indian population are clearly revealed in the Granth, as they found themselves helpless time and again before the Muslim emperors.

Thou art the river, all-knowing and all-seeing. How can I, a fish, find thy limits? ... Getting out of thee, I burst and die.
Ist (**25/1/85**)

The intoxicating herb of secular love has killed me, so does the remaining world fare (at its hands).
Ist (**61/1/208**)

Beholding this world on fire, I hastened and entered the Guru's sanctuary.
3rd (**70/1/237**)

Abandoning all devices and endeavours, I have sought the Guru's sanctuary.
5th (**71-72/1/242-3**)

The dark age is the scalpel, the kings are the butchers, and righteousness has taken wings and flown. In this no-moon night of

falsehood, the moon of truth is not seen to rise anywhere. In my search, I have become bewildered, I find no path ... says Nanak; by what means can the mortal be delivered?
Ist (**145**/1/483)

The desert is not satiated with rain and the hunger of fire is not quenched ... How many enquiries and interrogations should Nanak make regarding the true name? His hunger for it is never appeased.
Ist (**148-9**/1/495-6)

Having conquered *Khurasan*, Babar has terrified Hindustan. The creator takes not the blame on himself and has sent the *Mughal* as death's myrmidon. So much beating was inflicted that people shrieked. Didst thou, O God, feel no compassion?
Thou, O maker, equally art the master of all. If a mighty man smites another mighty man then the mind feels no anger. If a powerful tiger falling on a herd kills it, its master should show manliness. The dogs have spoiled and laid waste the priceless country. No one pays heed to the dead.
Ist (**360**/3/1200)

None knows what is to happen to him hereafter. The bewailer too rises up and departs.
5th (**885**/6/2882)

O saints, what means should I now adopt, by which all evil thoughts may be dispelled and the mind be steeped in meditation of the Lord?
9th (**902**/6/2938)

O my mother, whom should I tell of the pain that I have? Without my God, my soul cannot live. How can I still the pain, O my mother?
Ist (**990**/6/3245)

The primal Lord is called *Allah*; the turn of the Muslim divines has come. Tax is levied on the temples of gods. Such a practice has come into vogue. The ablution pots, calls to prayer and prayer carpets are seen everywhere and the Lord appears in the *blue** form. (*Blue was missed by the translation). In every house, all the persons say, '*Mian*', your language has become different, O men. If thou, O Lord, wishest to appoint *Mir Babar* the king of the earth; what power have I to challenge it?
Ist (**1191**/7/3926)

One cannot know the praises of the Lord of the world, O mother! Without seeing God, one cannot say aught regarding him. How can one describe him, O my mother? The Lord is high up in the sky and down below in the nether world as well. How can I describe him? Make thou me understand this thing.
Ist (**1256**/7/4143)

When none can withhold man from coming, then how can one hold him back from going?
*I*st (**1329/8/4385**)

What do I know about what the Lord does and causes to be done?
*I*st (**1331/8/4393**)

What power have I to utter the unutterable name of the Lord? If thou, O Lord, dost make me worship, then alone can I worship thee.
*I*st (**1331/8/4393**)

He who has created all this, alone understands its mystery.
5th (**1342/8/4427**)

When the Lord's will is so ordained, then to whom should I cry out?
*I*st (**1344/8/4436**)

5. Mysterious sayings of the Gurus

Sayings such as those which refer to a foetus praying to God raise questions as to the place of the consciousness when the same baby is born. When does the foetus become conscious of its pain in the womb?

According to another saying, by taking a dip in the tank of Ramdass (The Golden Temple), not only does one save oneself, but also one's whole posterity and one is absolved of all the sins of previous births.

It is said that God remains in darkness for thirty-six ages (yugas). This seems strange since God is the supreme light that enlightens the whole universe.

Other such mysterious sayings provoke more questions.

Air is the Guru, water the father, earth the great mother, and day and night, the two female and male nurses, in whose lap the entire world play is enacted.
*I*st (**8/1/27**)

From the true Lord, proceeded the air and from air came the water. From the water God created the three worlds and in every heart he infused his light.
*I*st (**19-20/1/64**)

They who are pleasing to thee, are good (in themselves). None is counterfeit or genuine.
*I*st (**61**/1/209)

With body reversed thou hast performed penance within and prayed to the master, O my merchant friend! Upside down thou hast said prayers unto the Lord with fixed attention and affection.
*I*st (**74-5**/1/253)

In the first watch of the night, O my merchant friend! God put the mortal into the womb.
He meditates on God, utters his name and on the name of the Lord God he reflects, O merchant friend! The Lord God's name he repeats and ponders on and in the womb's fire he sustains life by thinking of God.
*I*st (**76**/1/258)

Firstly, the one Lord created his own self, secondly, the sense of duality and thirdly the three-phased mammon.
3rd (**113**/1/374)

That Lord consort, on his couch enjoys the virtuous and chaste brides.
*I*st (**21-2**/1/72)

My maid, my beloved, is in every way playful. He ever enjoys the virtuous wife. Behold my plight (away from him).
*I*st (**23**/1/78)

By praising his name, the pious person reforms his life. He him-self is ever emancipated and saves all his lineage.
3rd (**86**/1/291)

Some deal in the true name through the love of *Gurbani*. They save themselves and save their entire lineage as well.
3rd (**117-118**/1/389)

The counterfeit and the genuine thou thyself has created. Thou thyself assayest all the mortals. Having assayed the true thou consignest them to thy treasury and the false thou misleadest in doubt.
3rd (**119**/1/393)

The holy man saves himself, saves his entire lineage and reforms his life too.
3rd (**125**/1/413)

The Guru's devoted Sikh is known in the four ages.
3rd (**125**/1/414)

Within the body are the two brothers, sin and virtue. Meeting together both have created the uni-verse.
3rd (**126**/1/417)

He swims across himself and saves his entire lineage. In the Lord's court he meets with no obstruc-tion.
3rd (**130-1**/1/433)

They who meditate on the master in the month of *Maghar* (November) are not born again.
5th (**135**/1/448)

Giving the intoxicating herb of worldly love to eat, thou thyself hast led astray the world.
2nd (**138-9**/1/459)

Thou hast created self-conceit and arrogance and infused avarice into mortals.
2nd (**139**/1/460)

He is saved himself along with his family and by giving the name of the Lord and master saves the whole world.
4th (**140**/1/463)

The great God *Shiva* searches for the man, who knows God. Nanak the *Brahm giani* himself, the exalted Lord.
5th (**261**/2/865-6)

The knower of God is the creator of the whole world.
5th (**273**/2/909)

He is the Sat-Guru who remembers the Lord. True it is, that the true Lord and true Guru are one.
4th (**304**/2/1014)

The men who act as the women tell them to are impure, filthy and foolish.
4th (**304**/2/1016)

He himself has created all women and men. God plays every part.
4th (**304**/2/1016)

My creator, thou thyself adorest the true Guru and causest others

to adore him.
4th (**311-2**/2/1040)

O saints, sublime is the tank of *Ram Dass*, whosoever bathes therein, his lineage is saved, his own soul is blessed as well. The world sings his praise. He obtains the boons of his heart's desire.
5th (**623**/4/2044)

By having ablution in the tank of *Ram Dass*, all the sins committed by the person, are washed away.
5th (**624**/4/2048)

By bathing in the tank of *Ram Dass*, all the sins previously committed are washed away.
5th (**625**/4/2053)

All his generations are emancipated in an instant and his filth of many births is washed away.
5th (**824**/5/2683)

My coming and going, doubt and dread, have fled and my sins of many births have been washed away.
5th (**824**/5/2685)

With peace, poise and pleasure, I sing the Lord's praises and my adversaries and villains are all destroyed.
5th (**829**/5/2698)

Meditating on the Lord, his slaves are ferried across the world ocean and their sins of many births are washed off.
5th (**865**/5/2818)

He is a swine, a dog, a donkey, a cat, a beast, a filthy one, a mean man and a *pariah* (low caste), who turns away his face from the Guru. He is made to wander in other existences.
Ist (**832**/5/2708)

When, in the middle of hopes, man remains without hope, then, O Nanak he meets the one Lord.
Ist (**877**/6/2855)

In the male is the female and in the female is the male. Realise thou this, O God divine.
Ist (**879**/6/2861)

No sensitiveness, no stupefaction, no water, no wind, no form and no world is there, where the true Guru is united with God and where the imperishable Lord and the unap-proachable master abide.
5th (**883**/6/2875)

No one dies, nor does anyone come and go.
5th (**885**/6/2883)

My halters (death nooses) of millions of births are hewed down.
5th (**893**/6/2910)

The compassionate Lord is the saviour of all. Contemplating the Lord, even for a moment, the sins of millions of births are eradicated.
5th (**894**/6/2913)

The sins of millions of births are eradicated. Remembering the

Lord master, pain does not touch man.
5th (**897**/6/2922)

First is the butter and afterwards the milk. The filth purifies the soap.
5th (**900**/6/2932)

In the *Kalage* (dark age), (semitic books) the Quran has become the approved book. The Brahmins, the Hindu religious books and *Puranas* are not esteemed. The merciful *Khuda* is now the name of the Lord, O Nanak.
Ist (**903**/6/2942)

Through self-conceit the world comes into being, O sire. Forgetting the name, it suffers pain and perishes.
Ist (**946**/6/3096)

God's slave saves himself and saves his ancestors as well. His associates are emancipated and then he ferries himself across.
Ist (**1026**/6/3365)

With head downwards in the mother's round belly, mortal man was wrapt in the Lord. Within the mother's belly, with every breath, man remembered the true name in his mind.
Ist (**1026-7**/6/3366)

By his order, God created ten incarnations and innumberable gods and numberless devils. In his will, the Lord spent thirty-six ages in seedless trance.
Ist (**1037**/6/3403)

Out of the formless Lord, have come the ten incarnations ... The Lord has made the gods, demons, heavenly heralds and celestial musicians. Everyone does the deed, writ in his destiny.
Ist (**1038**/6/3407)

Indras seated on their thrones are in fear of death. They do many deeds but *yama* spares them not.
3rd (**1049**/6/3448)

I have thought about *Brahma, Vishnu* and *Shiva*. They are bound down by the three dispositions, so salvation remains far from them.
3rd (**1049**/6/3448)

He who created *Brahma, Vishnu* and *Shiva*; he himself yokes each one to his task.
3rd (**1051**/6/3453)

He creates forms and creating enjoys their sight. As for himself, he worships himself.
5th (**1073**/6/3530)

Merits and demerits are the same, since they are created by the creator himself.
3rd (**1092**/6/3595)

Nanak utter thou the spell of '*He is me - and I am he*'. The three worlds are included in that Lord.
3rd (**1093**/6/3597)
Bathing in the dust of the Guru's feet, the filth of many births is washed off.
5th (**1097**/6/3611)

The judge, the preacher and the penitent shall all arise and depart. The spiritual leaders, prophets and apostles; none of these shall remain stable. The fasting, the call to prayer, the prayer and Muslim religious books; all shall vanish without knowing the Lord.
5th (**1100**/6/3623)

The banks of rivers, pilgrim stations, deities, temples at *Kedarnath, Mathura, Banaras* and thirty-three crores of gods along with *Indra* shall pass away. The *Smritis*, the *Shashtras*, the four *Vedas* and the six systems shall vanish away. The books, the songs, poems and poets too shall depart.
The celibates, the men of charity and solitude are all under the power of death.
5th (**1100**/6/3624)

It was an auspicious time when the great true Guru first arrived at *Kurukashetra*. The news spread through the worlds and beings of three worlds came to behold the Guru. The gods, men, silent sages and all of the three worlds came to behold him. They who received the touch of the perfect Guru, the true Guru, their sins were effaced and dispelled.
4th (**1116**/7/3676)

Sire Lord accomplishes the tasks of the saintly persons and he delivered the twenty-one generations of *Prahlad* the saint.
3rd (**1133**/7/3728-9)

If a man reflects on the Lord even for a moment, then he lives for ever and ever.
5th (**1204**/7/3970)

Enjoying the saint's society, even for a moment, one is blessed with millions of heavens.
5th (**1208**/7/3983)

There are millions of *Shashtras, Smritis* and *Puranas.* ... There are countless gods of water and countless mountains of gold. There are countless thousand hooded serpents who utter God's new names.
5th (**1236**/7/4073)

Adoring the Lord's name, the entire lineage and all generations are redeemed.
Ist (**1241**/7/4092)

For thirty-six ages (*Yugas*) the Lord abided in utter darkness. For such was his will.
3rd (**1282**/7/4230)

His utterance is approved in the Lord's court, who deems both poison and nectar alike.
Ist (**1328**/8/4382-3)

6. Guidelines for following the Guru

Water Used to Wash the Saint's Feet Should Be Drunk

Those who have exceedingly bad luck, cannot drink the water used to wash the dust from the saint's feet.
4th (**1325**/8/4371)

As long as there is breath in my mind, make me drink the water used to wash the dust from the saint's feet.
4th (**1326**/8/4376)

Shiva, Narad, the cobra king and the silent sages long to drink the water that washed the dust of the saint's feet.
4th (**1326**/8/4376)

Prostration at the Guru's Feet Commended

Therefore, make thou not even a moment's slothful delay. Go and fall at the saint's feet.
4th (**1326**/8/4377)

If some good man seeks good for himself, he should lie prostrate before the Guru.
4th (**1310**/8/4322)

The Guru at Whose Feet Prostration Should Not Be Made.

Fall not thou ever at the feet of him, who calls himself a Guru and a spiritual preceptor and goes begging.
I (**1245**/7/4108)

No Disrespect Should Be Shown to the Guru

Whosoever shows disrespect to the slave of the Lord, him the Lord destroys.
5th (**1235**/7/4071)

They whose eyes are attracted by the love of the Lord, behold the Lord God by contemplating his name. If the eyes see another, O slave Nanak, they ought to be gouged out.
4th (**1318**/8/4349)

If the ears hear not God's holy word, a block should be put in those ears ... The tongue, which utters not the name, ought to be cut out bit by bit.
5th (**1362**-3/8/4498)

8

PRAYERS IN THE GRANTH

Introduction

1. **Personal prayers for the name of God**

2. **Personal prayers for the vision of God**

3. **Personal prayers for salvation**

Introduction

The holy Granth can be called the book of prayers and praises to the creator God by the Gurus. The prayers, laudations and invocaions, magnifying the creator Lord can be found on almost every page of the Granth. The most adorable of such prayers is the hymn of laudation called "Aarti" by Guru Nanak.

Placed on the salver of heaven are the lamps, sun and moon, with pearls of constellations -
thy offering;
fragrant mountain breezes - thy incense,
the wind - thy fly whisk.
The entire blossoming vegetation, thy flower offering - thou who art light.
How wonderful is this *aarti* (worship). Thy *aarti*. Thou annuller of transmigration, divine spiritual harmony, thy worship orchestrates.
Thousands thy eyes, thy forms: yet without physical eyes formless thou remainest; thousands thy lotus feet, thy senses of fragrance - yet without visible organs are thou! Wonderful to me are thy ways. In all creation is thy light, thou who art light. In all creation shines thy effulgence - thou who art light. In thy light shines all that exists. By the master's word is this light made manifest. Submission to his will is the highest prayer offering.

My self yearns for a touch of thy lotus feet, fragrant, in thirst unquenchable. Grant to the Chatrik[i], O Nanak, the water of thy grace; in thy name grant him an abode.
Ist (**663**/4/2174-5)

The Gurus sung the praises of God, marvelling at his attributes. To this praise and worship they have added their personal and heartfelt petitions, to know him and his name and to see him with their eyes (vision) and to get rid of the pain of transmigration and merge with him.

We shall therefore produce quotations from their prayers in the following order:

1. Personal prayers for the name of God.

2. Personal prayers for the vision of God

3. Personal prayers for salvation.

---

[i] *Chatrik.* A bird with unquenchable thirst called Papiha.

1. Personal prayers for the name of God

These very real, heart-felt prayers of the Gurus are directed to the eternal God, the creator. By these prayers they want to obtain the appropriate name of God, in order to call upon him.

I an insect and a worm, have sought thy shelter, mercifully bestow on me the light of God's name, O true Guru! O my friend, the bright Guru! Illumine me with the name of the omnipresent Lord.
Ist (**9-10**/1/32)

Give pied cuckoo Nanak, the water of thy mercy, O God, so that he may have an abode in thy name.
Ist (**13**/1/42)

If I meet some holy friend, who points out to me the Lord, the treasure of virtues, I am quartered unto him, who reveals unto me the Lord's name.
4th (**39-40**/1/135-6)

Without God's name, I cannot sustain life, O my true Guru! Implant the name within me.
4th (**40**/1/136)

The name is an invaluable jewel. It is with the perfect Guru. The true Guru brings it out and gives the bright jewel of the name to him who is attached to his service.
4th (**40**/1/136)

My mind is athirst for God's name. May the Guru be pleased to grant that name to me.
4th (**40**/1/137)

The relish of the nectar of the immortal name is exquisitely fine. In what way can I obtain the nectar and taste it?
4th (**41**/1/139)

God himself is the relish of his name and he himself is the divine elixir. Showing his grace, God himself gives the nectar of the name to the virtuous and lets it trickle into his mouth.
4th (**41**/1/140-1)

Have mercy on Nanak, O Lord, and bless him with thy true name.
5th (**44-5**/1/151)

O my father! Give me the name of the Lord God as a gift and a dowry.
4th (**79**/1/265)

I am a minstrel of the Lord God, the master, and I have come to his gate. O my merciful master God! ever grant me the gift of meditating on thy name.
3rd (**91**/1/307)

Come and meet me, O my beloved, the life of the world. Be merciful, O Lord God and implant thy name in my heart.
4th (**95**/1/318)

O God! cause me to meet the society of the saints and the true persons. On meeting the congre-

gation of the pious, I shall ponder on God's name.
4th (**96**/1/320)

Thou, O Lord, art an ocean of water and I am thy fish. I, the thirsty pied-cuckoo, long for a drop of the water of thy name.
5th (**100**/1/334)

O my saintly Guru! grant Nanak the gift of the name of that unapproachable and unfathomable Lord.
5th (**102**/1/340)

Nanak's supplication is this: Show me thy benediction and grant me thy name. O God, the master and Lord, whose mansion is eternal, unite me with thee.
5th (**133**/1/441)

What is the penance by which I may become a penitent? What is that name by which the filth of pride may be washed away?
5th (**187**/2/623)

O the beneficent Lord of the meritless, my mind is engrossed in lust, wrath, avarice and worldly love. Show mercy unto Nanak and bless him with thy name. He is ever a sacrifice unto thee.
5th (**210**/2/695-6)

Meet me, O my Lord of the world, bestow on me thy name. Blasted and blighted is the love which is without the name.
5th (**240**/2/793)

I, a beggarly man, beg a gift af thee, O Lord! Show mercy and grant me thy name.
5th (**289**/2/963)

Nanak prays for thy name, O God, show thy mercy and unite me with thyself.
5th (**317**/2/1057)

O father, I have seen that the world is poison. Preserve me, O Lord of the universe. Thy name is my support.
5th (**381**/3/1269)

Hear thou, O Lord, the supplication of Nanak. Into his mind infuse thy name.
5th (**389**/3/1292)

Thy doings seem sweet unto me. Nanak craves for the wealth of God's name.
5th (**394**/3/1307)

I make supplication in the presence of the perfect Guru. Nanak craves for the capital of the wealth of God's name.
5th (**395**/3/1312)

Shower thy benediction on me, O Lord, that Nanak may obtain thy name.
5th (**408**/3/1351)

The saint's tongue repeats the Lord's name. This I have heard is the only way to emancipation. In the dark age, difficult to obtain is the Lord in the world.
5th (**409**/3/1357)

They age not, die not and fall not into hell, who meditate on God's name.
1st (**438**/3/1446)

Meet me in the society of saints and rescue me, O my master. With clasped hands, I make supplication before thee, O Lord and master! Grant me thy name. By thy grace, O Lord, I ask for thy name, fall at thy feet and shed my self-conceit. O Lord, the embodiment of compassion, take pity on me, that I may remain in thy refuge and wander not elsewhere.
5th (**457**/3/1508)

I, an insect and a worm, have sought thy shelter. Mercifully bestow on me, the light of God's name, O true Guru.
4th (**492**/3/1624)

O my brother, let someone, who may implant God's name in me, come and meet me. My life, my soul and body and all I have, I give to my beloved, who may narrate to me the divine discourse of my Lord God.
4th (**494**/3/1630)

O my beloved Lord, show mercy and unite me with thee and through thy kindness attach me to thy skirt. Bless me with thy name that I may meditate on it, O Lord.
5th (**545**/4/1793)

I am a helpless being and all the ages through, thou art the beneficent Lord. Reveal thou, thy name unto me. O my beloved

Lord, show thou mercy unto me. Unite me in union with the munificent, true Guru and bless me with the support of thy name, O Lord!
3rd (**603**/4/1983)

As the fish perishes without water, so I die without the name. O my master, by thy grace, bless me with the water of God's name. Within my mind day and night, I crave for the name.
4th (**607**/4/1995)

To repeat the Lord God's name is the yearning, I long for. O God, have mercy on me the forest dweller. The Lord God is the raindrop and I, a sparrow hawk, am wailing and bewailing for it. O Lord God, my master, shower thy benediction on me and pour into my mouth the raindrop of thy name, even for a trice.
4th (**668**/4/2189)

O my Lord, do thou save me. Of myself, I can do nothing, O my Lord. Mercifully, bless me with thy name.
5th (**675**/4/2212)

Lord, merciful to the meek, take pity on me, that I may ignore the supreme attractions of mammon. O Lord, make thy slave's arduous toil fruitful and bless him with thy name, for by remembering it, he sustains his life.
5th (**683**/4/2235)

O God, the Lord of the world and destroyer of pain, I seek the

refuge of thy feet. Bless thou me, thy serf, with thy name. O Lord show mercy unto me, save me by thy grace and taking me by the arm, pull me out of the well.
5th (**683**/4/2236-7)

Is there any devotee, who is detached from worldly valuables, who can water my mind with the nectar of the name?
5th (**687**/4/2248)

Nanak asks for the gift of God's name. O my merciful master, mercifully grant it to me ... Nanak begs a boon. Mercifully bless me with thy name.
5th (**710**/4/2323)

O thou, the compassionate and kind Lord master, merciful to the meek, I seek thy refuge. Take pity on Nanak, O God, and bless him with thy name and the dust of the saint's feet.
5th (**750**/5/2444-5)

Bless me with an abode in thy name that my soul may be pacified.
Ist (**753**/5/2453)

In this age, emancipation is obtained only through the Lord's name.
Ist (**768**/5/2501)

Completely burn up my greed and avarice and grant me the support of the Lord's name.
Ist (**790**/5/2574)

I am a beggar at thy door, O God, praying for alms. In thy mercy, bless thou me with it. Unite me thy slave, with the supreme Guru, that I may obtain thy name, O God.
Ist (**790**/5/2575)

The world is a well of poison. In it is the pitch darkness of spiritual ignorance and worldly love. Hold me by the hand and save me, O my Lord. Bless me with thy name, O God.
5th (**837**/5/2727)

With folded hands, Nanak asks for the gift of the true name. My master, bless thou me, with thy grace, in thy will.
Ist (**844**/5/2750)

Says Nanak, shower thou thy benediction on me, O Lord. For me, the blind man, thy name is the staff.
5th (**847**/5/2761)

My Lord, bless thou Nanak with the greatness of the gift of thy name and the dust of the feet of thy saintly persons.
5th (**916**/6/2988)

Nanak prays, my Lord, take pity on me, so that I may live contemplating thy name.
5th (**926**/6/3017)

Is there any such friend or intimate of mine, who could ever recite to me the Lord's name?
5th (**980**/6/3212)

Nanak is ever a sacrifice unto thee, O Lord. Bless me with thy name.
5th (**988**/6/3238)

O father, I am false and destined for ill. Thy name I have not obtained. My mind is blind and has gone astray in doubt.
Ist (**989**/6/3241)

O Lord of the universe, what is thy name like and how can it be known? If thou dost call me into thy presence, I would ask thee one thing: how can mortal man become one with thee?
Ist (**992**/6/3252)

God and God's name are dear unto me. *Correct rendering would be "I am separated from God and his name".* Let someone come and unite me with him, O my mother.
4th (**996**/6/3263)

Servant Nanak has entered thy sanctuary, O my God. Be thou merciful and merge me with thy name.
4th (**997**/6/3267)

Unite me with the society of saints and bless me with the honour and credit of thy name.
4th (**997**/6/3268)

Humble Nanak begs for thy name, that purges him of duality and doubt.
5th (**1005**/6/3294)

Lowly Nanak asks for alms at thy door. Bless him with the greatness of thy name.
Ist (**1021**/6/3347)

Nanak tells the truth, that he asks from the Lord alone; O Lord of the will, bless me with thy true name.
Ist (**1024**/6/3358)

Mercifully bless me with thy ambrosial name and the jewel of the lamp of the Guru's gnosis.
Ist (**1039**/6/3409-10)

How can a perverse person obtain knowledge of the Lord's name? Without knowledge of the name, man continues coming and going.
Ist (**1042**/6/3421)

O Lord, do thou thyself, unite me with thee, though I am but a sinking stone. Ever eternal is thy true name.
3rd (**1048**/6/3444)

Keep me ever in the society of saints and bless me with the gift of this name of thine.
5th (**1074**/6/3547)

I ask for the dust from the saint's feet, that I may be blessed with the supreme status and be rid of the filth of many births. Chronic diseases are cured by the medicine of the Lord's name. I crave to be imbued with blessing of the immaculate Lord.
5th (**1080**/6/3551)

O creator, my beloved Lord, hear my supplication and bless me with thy name.
5th (**1085**/6/3570)

O Lord, I have sought thy refuge. Save my honour and bless me with thy true name.
Ist (**1274**/7/4202)

Throughout the eight watches, Nanak sings thy praise, O God, and begs from thee the gift of thy name alone.
5th (**1302**/8/4297)

O benevolent Lord, show mercy and compassion unto me. O Lord, Nanak begs thee, for the bounty of thy name.
5th (**1305-6**/8/4309)

So Lord, show mercy and kindness unto me and mercifully attach me to thy name. Mercifully lead me on to the true Guru, for by meeting with the true Guru, I shall dwell upon thy name, O my master.
4th (**1309**/8/4319)

O compassionate God, thou Lord and master, bless me with the bounty of thy name. Thy slaves and saints ever beg thee for it.
4th (**1315**/8/4340)

O my merciful Lord God, bless me with the gift of thy name and save the honour of thy slave.
4th (**1316**/8/4342)

O my Lord God, slave Nanak asks for the gift of the support of thy name alone.
4th (**1317**/8/4350)

I have no concern with any other water. O God, bless thou me, the pied-cuckoo, with a drop of the nectar of thy name.
5th (**1321**/8/4360)

O Lord, take pity on thy slave Nanak and bless him with thy name, of whose magnificence there is no equal.
5th (**1323-4**/8/4368)

O creator Lord, thou alone art my almsgiver. I ask for but one boon from thee. Bless thou me, O Lord, with thy name.
Ist (**1329**/8/4384-5)

2. Personal prayers for the vision of God

Gurus, like other religious persons, have a great longing to see God with their own eyes. They were ready to make great sacrifices, if only they could obtain a glimpse of the creator for a moment. However they could only have subjective experience of God in the tenth gate of their mind, where God comes to stay, according to the Sikh faith.

Thy devotees are ever hungry for thee, O God! Fulful my desires, O giver of peace! Grant me a sight of thee and take me into thine embrace.
Ist (**74**/1/251)

Seeking and searching for thee, O my master, I have grown desirous of the sight of thee.
5th (**98**/1/326)

To see God, O Nanak, my soul craves and my mind is thirsty. I touch the feet of him, who may unite me with the master in the month of *Chetar* (March).
5th (**133-4**/1/441-2)

In *Assu* (September) the Lord's love is overflowing from within me. How shall I go and meet God? Within my mind and body is

a great thirst for the sight of the Lord. Let someone come and cause me to meet him, O mother!
5th (**135**/1/446)

O Lord, grant me a sight of thee. My hope is in thee. My God show mercy unto me and fulfil my desire.
4th (**164**/2/550)

The longing for God is ever within my mind and heart. O God, how shall I see thee?
4th (**167**/2/558)

Show mercy and cause me to see thee, O God. Within my soul and body is this great yearning.
4th (**170**/2/570)

How shall I see the Lord, my master, the yearning of my soul and body?
4th (**175**/2/584)

To see the vision of God, my soul remembers him. In thirst and hope of seeing my Lord, day and night I think of him. Is there any saint, who may immediately unite me with him?
5th (**204**/2/678)

Wandering through many existences in several births, I suffered torture again and again. By thy grace, I have obtained a human body. Now grant me a view of thee, O my God, the king.
5th (**207**/2/687)

Though virtueless, I make my supplication, O sovereign Lord: bless me with a sight of thee.
5th (**241**/2/799)

The wife has grown weak through grief at separation from her spouse She has grown thin in sorrow for her spouse saying, "How shall I she see him with mine eyes?"
5th (**242**/2/800)

I thirst for the feet of the Lord and long to see him. I look for him in all places.
5th (**249**/2/825)

O Lord, save Nanak with those who are desirous of a sight of thee alone.
5th (**262**/2/870)

For the sake of the sight of God, the friend, my soul has become sad.
4th (**369**/3/1230)

Great is my mind's desire to have a sight of him. Is there any such saint, who will cause me to meet my beloved?
5th (**375**/3/1246-7)

My soul thirsts for a vision of thee; thus absorbed in thy love, I abide in equipoise and bliss.
5th (**389**/3/1292)

Pondering and contemplating over God's name, man never repents. Nanak thirsts for the sight of thee, fulfil his desire, O Lord.
5th (**398**/3/1320)

Standing and sitting. I cannot live without him. I search for the way to a vision of him.
5th (**401**/3/1330)

With clasped hands Nanak craves for a boon, O God, bless thy saints with the sight of thee.
5th (**406**/3/1346)

Though man may read *smiritis* and *shastras* and perform many rit-uals, without the vision of thee, O Lord, there is no peace.
5th (**408**/3/1351)

It is long, long, long, long since my soul felt a great thirst for thee, O God. Show me thyself and appraise me of thy presence.
5th (**408**/3/1353)

Thou art the giver, I am thy beggar. My God, grant me a sight of thee.
*I*st (**419**/3/1390)

For a sight of the Lord, I have a great thirst and I think of him in many a way. Be merciful, O my transcendent Lord, show mercy to me, O God, the enemy of pride.
5th (**431**/3/1422)

How shall I find the Guru, by clinging to whom, I can see my beloved. O, bounteous God, cause me to meet the supreme Guru. Through the Guru alone, I can unite with thee.
4th (**452**/3/1490)

Show mercy my Lord and grant me a vision of thee. Thy praises I

sing night and day. With my hair, I cleanse the feet of thy slave. This is my life's object.
5th (**500**/3/1647)

Have mercy on me and show me a vision of thee, O Guru. Through the name, I have burnt down my ego.
1st (**504**/3/1662)

With mine eyes I have seen the Lord's light, but my great thirst, to behold him, quenches not.
5th (**577**/4/1497)

Be merciful and show me a vision of thee. Bless me with such a gift, O Lord.
3rd (**666**/4/2185)

Day and night I thirst for the vision of the Lord and ever think of him daily.
5th (**703**/4/2299)

Give me intelligence concerning the beloved. I will sever my head and place it before him, if he shows me a sight of him, even for a moment.
5th (**703**/4/2299)

O Lord, show me thy face even for a trice and I shall not give my mind to another.
5th (**708**/4/2316)

My mind desires thee. Let me have a vision of thee, that my anxiety may depart.
5th (**708**/4/2318)

Tell me the time when I shall obtain my Lord? Auspicious is that moment and destiny, when I shall attain to the Lord of the world. My mind thirsts for the sight of the Lord. Unto him Nanak is a sacrifice.
5th (**709**/4/2319)

My mother, my mind thirsts for the Lord. I cannot live, even for a moment without my beloved. Within my mind is the desire to see a vision of him.
5th (**716**/4/2341)

My hands are the begging bowl and I hunger for a vision of thee, O God. Day by day, I beg at thy door to see thee. I make a beggar's cry. Bless thou me, the beggar at thy door, with alms, O Lord.
1st (**721**/4/2354)

Roaming and rambling, I returned and even then I saw not my spouse. In what way can this poor soul of mine take courage?
5th (**737**/5/2404)

What service shall I render thee? What should I say to please thee? In what way can I see a vision of thee, O my Lord?
5th (**738**/5/2406)

All long for the vision of the Lord. Through good and perfect destiny the vision of the Lord is obtained.
5th (**745**/5/2428)

Let someone come and make me meet my darling beloved. For the sake of seeing the Lord, I will sell myself to him.
4th (**757/5/2467**)

Poor Nanak has gone mad for a sight of thee, O God.
4th (**757/5/2468**)

My master, make my feet tread thy way and my eyes see thee ... O, my spouse, look thou with grace on me, even for an instant and bless me with a vision of thee, that I may revel in thy love.
5th (**760/5/2479**)

By fearing the immaculate God, my Lord and master and by singing his praise, I behold him face to face.
4th (**773/5/2520**)

O, my beloved Lord, have mercy on me, that with my eyes, I may see thee.
5th (**780/5/2541-2**)

For the sight of the Lord, my mind greatly thirsts. Says Nanak, O God, I seek nothing but thy protection.
5th (**805/5/2621**)

When shall I see my Lord with the delight of my soul? Better than waking is the dream, where I abide with my master.
5th (**816/5/2657-8**)

Hearing the *shastras* on four castes and four stages of life, my

thirst for the sight of the Lord is not sated.
5th (**816/5/2658**)

Beggar Nanak prays for the vision of the Lord and wishes to be blessed with the dust of the saints' feet.
5th (**824/5/2684**)

I go about searching all the country and foreign lands, as with-in my mind there is a great yearn-ing to see my Lord.
4th (**836/5/2721**)

In every particle of my body and mind is the pang of separation. Without seeing my Lord, I cannot sleep.
4th (**836/5/2723**)

My soul thirsts for thy love and vision, O Lord of the universe. Fulfil this desire of mine.
5th (**838/5/2728**)

O God, thy slave Nanak lives by beholding thee. Let me see thy face, even for a moment and a trice.
4th (**848/5/2767**)

Like a thirsty man without water, my soul yearns deeply for the vision of the Lord.
4th (**861/5/2805**)

May I obtain the gift of ever seeing thee and meeting with thee, O Lord!
5th (**862/5/2807**)

Thirsty with desire, I wander thinking, when shall I behold my Lord? O Nanak, is there any friendly holy man, who may unite me with my master?
5th (**928**/6/3026)

Searching for his vision, I wander thinking, when shall I meet my Lord, the treasure of all virtues?
5th (**928**/6/3026-7)

In search of the saints, I have become a hermit. For the sake of the vision of the Lord, I have adopted this costume.
Ist (**835**/6/3069)

Serf Nanak asks for but one boon, O Lord! Bless me with a vision of thee, for I love thee heartily.
5th (**959**/6/3145)

Within my mind, I thirst for a vision of the Lord and I am the handmaiden of his lotus feet.
5th (**964**/6/3161)

My Lord, how can I know what pleases thee? Within my mind is a great thirst to see thee. What kind of yoga, what knowledge and contemplation and what virtues please thee, O my master?
5th (**978**/6/3206)

O my spouse, I arise early to behold thee. Collyrium, garland, betel and dainties; all such relishes are but dust without seeing thee, O Lord.
5th (**1094**/6/3601)

My soul thou art fascinated, when shall I behold thee, O my love?
5th (**1094**/6/3602)

I am ardent to see thee, O Lord. What kind of face is thine ?
5th (**1096**/6/3610)

I ask for bounty from the Lord of the world, by which my hunger may be satiated. My venerable Lord, bless me, thy bard with a vision of thee, with which I may be sated.
5th (**1097**/6/3612)

My mind longs to meet my God. How can I behold his vision? I would deem it to be like obtaining lakhs of rupees, if thou, O Lord, shouldst talk to me even for an instant. ... Show me the path, O saints; how can I meet my Lord?
5th (**1098**/6/3616)

Standing at the door, O Lord, Nanak longs for thy vision.
Ist (**1187**/7/3914)

Within my mind is a thirst like that of the pied cuckoo for water. When shall I have a fruitful vision of the true Guru?
5th (**1202**/7/3963)

By the Guru's instruction, slave Nanak has obtained his Lord. My God, bless me with a vision of thee, for my mind yearns for it.
5th (**1202**/7/3964)

Showing his mercy the Lord has made me his own and within me has welled up a thirst to see him.
5th (**1227-8**/7/4045)

My mind greatly thirsts for the vision of the Lord. O luminous Lord, the Guru of the universe, meet thou with Nanak.
5th (**1304-5**/8/4305-6)

What is the way, by which I may obtain a vision of thee, O Lord? O Lord, I hope and thirst for a wish-fulfilling vision of thee. My mind craves to see thee.
5th (**1305**/8/4306)

O mother, slave Nanak's mind craves to see his Lord God and he would meet with him, if the Guru be merciful to him.
4th (**1315**/8/4341)

3. Personal prayers for salvation

As mentioned before, salvation according to the Sikh faith means getting rid of the bondage of birth and rebirth by merging into God, where one's light merges with the supreme light and one's identity is lost. Salvation is not very easy to obtain, because of the writ of God written on every forehead, based on previous deeds, which cannot be erased. It is by good luck and by the grace of God that a human being can meet a true Guru, who reveals the name which leads to salvation.

I am poor and humble but I am thine, O Lord God! Save me, save me, O thou greatest of the great.
4th (**13**/1/43)

My soul and body are thine and thou art my master. Rid me of ego and merge me with thee.
Ist (**20**/1/66)

Come and meet me 'my maids' and unite me with my beloved.
3rd (**38**/1/129)

I go and ask those friends the way, by which the Lord is to be met and introduced. I am foolish and ignorant and have sought thy sanctuary. Take pity on me and unite me with God.
4th (**39**/1/134)

Ever standing up, I enquire the way to my Lord. If someone shows me the way, I will go to him. I follow in the footsteps of those who have enjoyed my beloved. I beseech them and entreat them. I have a yearning to meet my master. My fellow brother! Let someone unite me in union with my Lord God.
4th (41/1/138)

Within my soul and body is a very great hunger for God. Let someone come and unite me with him, O my mother! I have searched (for him) in four directions. Without the spouse there is no other place of rest.
5th (49/1/166)

Let someone come and introduce me to God, rejuvenator of my very life. I cannot live without seeing my darling. The tears are falling profusely from my eyes.
4th (94/1/315)

If by greatest good fortune some friendly saint were to meet me, he would show me the way to the Lord God, my beloved ... I search and seek in my heart and body. How shall I meet my amiable beloved, O my mother?
4th (94-5/1/316)

He alone is a friend, comrade, beloved and brother of mine, who shows* me the way to the lion man, the incarnation of God. (*The correct rendering of the original should be "who may show" me the way to the lion man, the incarnation of God.)
4th (95/1/317)

When shall I now meet thee, O my beloved, auspicious Lord?
5th (97/1/322)

Clasping both my hands, I make supplication, O Lord! Show mercy to me and save this sinking stone.
5th (103/1/342)

I have come and entered thy sanctuary. As it pleases thee, so do thou unite me with thyself.
5th (104-5/1/347)

O omnipotent Lord, show mercy and unite us with thyself, who on account of deeds done are separated from thee. Weary of wandering in all four directions, we have come to thy sanctuary, O Lord!
(Note: The stanza is actually meant to be singular but is written in the eastern poetic style where great people use "we" in place of "I".)
5th (133/1/440)

Nanak makes supplication before the Lord: Come and unite me with thee, O Lord!
5th (134/1/442)

Forsaking my self-conceit, I seek the Lord's refuge and with my mouth I utter sweet words. From many births, I am separated from thee, O God, my friend and re-

lation. Now mercifully unite me
with thyself.
5th (**136-7**/1/452)

Without God, the spouse, solace
is not obtained. I have searched
and seen all the spheres. My own
evil actions have kept me away
from the Lord. Why should I
accuse others? Show mercy, O
Lord, and save me. There is no
other bestower of mercy.
5th (**137**/1/452)

My sins are as innumerable as the
drops of water with which the
seas and oceans are filled. Show
me mercy and extend a little pity
and keep me, a sinking stone,
afloat.
Ist (**156**/2/523)

Serf Nanak asks for the dust of
their feet, those who have
obtained the true Guru.
3rd (**163-4**/2/547)

I am ignorant, O my all pervading
God, do thou accomplish my salvation.
4th (**166**/2/555)

I am a sinner, O my all pervading
Lord. I have taken refuge and
fallen at thy gate, O God! My
intellect is utterly without merit, I
am filthy. Sometime show mercy
to me too.
4th (**167**/2/558)

O my omnipresent Lord God,
such are my base actions. O my
meritorious Lord and master,

show me compassion and pardon
all my sins.
4th (**167**/2/560)

I know nothing of the past, nor do
I know anything regarding the
future. As God keeps me, so do I
stand. I am filled with short-
comings and mistakes. My Guru
take pity on me. Serf Nanak is
known as thy dog.
4th (**171**/2/571)

I am poor and humble and I am
thine, O Lord God. Save me, save
me, O thou greatest of the great.
4th (**171**/2/572)

Who is the benefactor, who may
take my hand and help me reach
his mansion?
5th (**181**/2/604)

What is the worship that I may
perform? What service can I do,
by which I may cross the terrible
ocean?
5th (**187**/2/623)

O my strong-armed and powerful
Lord, the ocean of peace, I am
falling into the pit. Take me by
the hand. My ears have no sense,
my eyes are not beautiful and are
afflicted and crippled. I cry at thy
door.
5th (**203**/2/674)

Give me the prop of thy hand, O
Lord, cherisher of the world, and
take me out of the pit.
5th (**203**/2/675)

By what means can I meet my master, the king and the Lord of the world? Is there any such saint, the giver of equipoise and peace, who may show me the way to the master?
5th (**204**/2/679)

O saviour, the five quarrelsome vices are the enemies of the soul, poor soul. Save me from them. They cause me suffering and annoy me immensely, so I have sought thy shelter ... I have grown weary of adopting many and various means, but in no way do they leave me.
5th (**206**/2/682-3)

O Lord of my life, show me mercy and compassion. Patronless, I have entered thy sanctuary, O master! From the blind well, take me out by giving me thy hand. I have no wisdom and skill whatever.
5th (**208**/2/691)

Thy secret, thou alone knowest, O my Guru. Thou art the all pervading creator Lord. Keep me, a helpless orphan, under thy protection and deliver me from my bondage.
5th (**209**/2/692)

The night is dark and gloomy, by what way may morning dawn upon me? I have grown weary by wandering and roaming about ... Adopting various ways I have searched for the Lord.
5th (**212**/2/703)

By hearing of the frightful path, I am terribly terrified. I have sought the asylum of the saints. O God's favourite, do thou save me.
5th (**240**/2/795)

My master, have pity and unite me, a fool and a sinner, with the society of the Guru, by clinging to which, I may swim across the sea of life.
5th (**250**/2/826-7)

I surrender my soul, I surrender my entire body, and I surrender all my lands. I offer my head to any dear friend, *who gives me the message of the Lord.
("who may give me" the message of the Lord, is a more correct rendering of the text).
5th (**247**/2/818)

I dedicate my body, soul and wealth unto him who may unite me with my master.
5th (**256**/2/850)

O, thou pardoner, pardon me and float Nanak across the ocean of the world.
5th (**260**/2/865)

Deep is the terrible ocean. The limits thereof cannot be found. I have no boat, nor any raft. I am drowning, save me, O my saviour king.
1st (**433**/3/1429)

My Lord God, shower thy benediction upon me, a stone. Ferry me across and peacefully pull me out

of the ocean. I am stuck in the mire of worldly affection and I am sinking. O Lord God, let me take hold of thy arm.
4th (**446**/3/1472)

My omnipotent, ineffable, infinite and immaculate Lord, hear thou this my supplication. With clasped hands, Nanak asks for this boon. O Lord, mercifully end my comings and goings (transmigration).
5th (**457**/3/1508)

I am a sinner, unwise, meritless, vile, stupid, stone-hearted, of low lineage, entangled in the mud of worldly love and stuck in the filth of doubt and of acts of egotism and egoism. The idea of death does not enter my mind. Through spiritual ignorance, I cling to the pleasure of woman and to the joy of mammon. My youth is wearing away and old age is progressing. Death, my companion, is counting or beholding my days ... I have wandered through many births, and have suffered the pain of many existences. Deeming revelry and gold to be sweet, I have become entangled with them. I have come thus far after wandering in many existences with immense loads of sin and have roamed through many foreign lands.
5th (**458**/3/1509)

I have passed through many births and deaths. But without union with my beloved, no salvation is

obtained. With folded hands Nanak has entered thy sanctuary. O my very powerful Lord, emancipate me.
5th (**462**/3/1522)

O Lord, merciful to the poor and perfectly blissful, I beg the dust from the feet of thy saints. False is worldly love, filthy the desire and evil the longing for it. Save me from these, remove doubt from my mind and redeem me, O form-less Lord.
Ist (**508**/3/1674)

O my soul, without God I obtain no peace, as the pied cuckoo cries out without the raindrops.
4th (**538**/4/1771)

I make efforts to meet my God, but no effort of mine works. Unsteady is the mind and unstable the wealth without my beloved. In no way am I consoled. Night and day, I crave and thirst for him. I cannot live without him, even for a moment. As a virtueless, unhonoured and orphaned bride, I supplicate thee. Meet me, O Lord, the treasury of mercy.
5th (**542**/4/1784)

I am foolish, stupid, masterless, restless, powerless, mean and insensate. Supplicates Nanak, I have sought thy refuge, O Lord. Save me from comings and goings.
5th (**543**/4/1786)

Supplicates Nanak, be merciful and meet me, O Lord, dear unto

my life. I have practised worship, penance and fasts to see thy feet, O Lord. But the mind's fire is never quenched, without the refuge of my Lord and master. My master, I have sought thy shelter; put off my fetters and ferry me across the ocean of the world.
5th (**545**/4/1793)

O creator, the cherisher of all hearts, rescue me from the world's blind well ... O God, master of the universe and merciful to the meek, stretch out thy hand and redeem me, beseeches Nanak.
5th (**546**/4/1797)

Thou art ever omnipotent, I am a meek beggar at thy door, O Lord. O God, the enemy of pride, save me. I am lost in love of worldly valuables. Bound by avarice, worldly love and vice, I have committed many misdeeds ... Show kindness to me, O purifier of sinners. I have grown weary of wandering through many existences.
5th (**547**/4/1799)

He who gives me the message of my Lord God, to him I offer my soul and body. I daily wave a fan over him, perform his service and carry water for him.
4th (**561**/4/1846)

Within me is the desire to meet my beloved. How can I attain to my perfect Guru? Even though hundreds of amusements be offered to a child, it cannot live without milk. My inner hunger departs not, O my spouse, even though I be served with hundred of dishes. Within my soul and body is the love of my beloved. How can my heart be comforted without seeing him. Hear, O my friend and brother, help me meet my intimate, the giver of peace ... I cannot live without him, even for a moment. I cry for the Lord as the pied cuckoo does for water.
5th (**564**/4/1853)

May someone come and cause me to meet my perfect true Guru. My soul and body, I shall dedicate to him. Cutting my body into bits, I shall offer these as well to him.
5th (**572**/4/1880)

I am a pied cuckoo, I am a meek pied cuckoo and I make supplication before my Lord. O Lord, make me meet my Guru, my beloved Guru.
5th (**574**/4/1886)

Show mercy, O God, and save me by thy grace. I am a sinner, I am a meritless sinner, but all the same I am a meek slave of thine.
4th (**575**/4/1888)

I am a wicked sinner and a great hypocrite. Thou art my immaculate and formless Lord. Prays Nanak, hear me, O my lord, save me, a sinking stone.
1st (**596**/4/1960)

With millions of sins this soul is enveloped. What then can man say? O Lord, Nanak, thy meek

slave, has entered thy asylum.
Write off all his debts.
5th (609/4/2001)

I am meritless, low, friendless and
sinful. I long for the shelter of the
saints. I am drowning in the blind
well of domestic love. O Lord,
stand by Nanak and save him.
5th (610/4/2005)

O, omnipresent Lord, merciful to
the meek and destroyer of
sorrows, without thee I have no
other shelter. Extricate me from
the ocean of the world, O Lord!
Nanak has entered thy sanctuary.
5th (616/4/2023)

My beloved, make me meet the
Guru, the friend of God. Meeting
with him, I shall inquire from him
the way to thee. I will sacrifice
myself to the friend who shows
me the path to God.
3rd (647/4/2123)

My soul is afraid, to whom should
I complain?
Ist (660/4/2164)

In what way can I meet with my
true master, O my mother?
Ist (661/4/2167)

I am a sinner, sinking in water
like a stone. Be merciful and
ferry me across.
3rd (666/4/2185)

I am ignorant and have trifling
and paltry understanding. Save
me by thy innate nature. I seek
thy protection. Thou alone art my

hope and a comforting friend. O
merciful master, my saviour, save
Nanak, the slave of thy house.
5th (674/4/2208)

Is there anyone, who can deliver
me of my bonds, unite me with
my Lord, read aloud to me the
Lord God's name and render this
mind stable and steady, so that it
does not wander anywhere again?
Is there any such friend to me? I
would give him my life and heart
and chattels and dedicate to him
my soul as well.
5th (674/4/2209)

O my friend, the enemy of pride,
be thou thy slave's succour. Take
me by the hand and rescue me.
5th (680/4/2231)

What effort should I make now,
by which my mental anxiety may
be ended and I may cross the
terrible ocean?
9th (685/4/2242)

He who in the twinkling of an eye
saves millions, mercifully make
me meet such a Guru, O my
beloved. I look to thy refuge, O
saint Guru, save me by giving me
thy hand and mercifully unite me
with God, the king. I have
wandered through various births
but have not found stability
anywhere. I serve my Guru, fall
at his feet and say: Pray show me
the way to my Lord, O Lord of
the world.
Ist (686/4/2247)

Is there any bestower of peace, who may recite to me the Lord's discourse? I shall be emancipated by meeting him.
5th (**687**/4/2249)

Grown weary, I have fallen at thy door, O Lord, and have firmly grasped thy support. O Lord, pull thy slave Nanak out of the world's well of fire.
5th (**701**/4/2294)

My erring soul is entangled with mammon. Whatever deeds I do are attached to avarice. I have bound myself to them all. I do not obtain understanding, I am engrossed in sinful pleasures and I have forgotten the praises of God. The fear of death has entered my mind and I cling to thy refuge, O ocean of mercy. I am a great sinner, stupid and greedy, but I have now grown weary of committing sins. The fear of death I do not forget. Anxiety has wasted my body away. I have been running about in ten directions, making efforts to obtain emancipation.
9th (**702**/4/2297-8)

How many of my misdeeds should I count? They are innumerable. Countless sins and errors have I committed; day by day, I always go wrong. I am inebriated with worldly valuables. By thy grace, can I be redeemed? In secrecy, I commit agonising sins, but the Lord is the nearest of the near. O Lord, show me mercy

and pull me out of the whirlpool of this world's dreadful ocean.
5th (**704**/4/2302)

Unite me with thyself, O my merciful master. I have fallen at thy door. Preserve me, O merciful to the meek. Wandering, I have become very weary. Take me by the hand, O beneficent Lord and ferry me across the ocean of the world. What should I say regarding my baseness? I am entangled in the love of gold and of woman and have not sung the Lord's praises. Night and day, I remain absorbed in worldly possessions and my mind's filth forsakes me not.
9th (**718**/4/2346)

I will surrender my wealth, riches and property, to him who can unite me with God my friend.
4th (**719**/4/2349)

Says Nanak, hear my supplication, O Lord, and emancipate me, the filthy, restless and lustful one.
5th (**738**/5/2407)

O my Lord, hear the supplication of Nanak, and deliver me, a sinking stone.
5th (**741**/5/2416)

Separated from thee, I have terribly suffered for many births. Now hold my hand, O sovereign, beloved Lord.
1st (**750**/5/2446)

Before whom should I untie the bundle that contains my pains, when everyone is brimful with woes. The whole world is filled with miseries, who then can know my inmost state?
Suhi I (**767**/5/2498)

O God, bless me with the dust of the feet of the perfect Guru, that I, the sinner, may be emancipated.
3rd (**772**/5/2516)

I surrender my soul and body unto the true Guru, that he may unite me with my Lord, the treasury of excellences.
4th (**776**/5/2526)

The Lord is merciful to the meek. Thou dost ferry thy devotees across the ocean of the world. Save me, a sinner, from my sins.
4th (**799**/5/2602)

Mortal man loves what he sees. How can I meet thee, whom I do not see, O my imperishable Lord? Show me mercy and put me on thy path, and tie me to the skirts of the society of saints, O Lord.
5th (**801**/5/2609)

I have no skill and wisdom, nor have I any service to my credit. Preserve me from doubt and dread and worldly attachment and cut away the noose of death, O my Lord.
5th (**811**/5/2640)

He is imbued with lust, wrath, avarice and slander, and has abandoned truth and contentment.

Pull me out of these, O my Lord. I have grown weary of these and have entered thy sanctuary. Nanak prays to thee, O Lord, save me pauper that I am, through the society of the saints.
5th (**820**/5/2672)

Hide thou my faults, O my Guru-God. As a sinner I have sought refuge at thy feet.
5th (**828**/5/2694)

O, my enticer, I do not sleep but continue sighing. I am adorned with necklaces, garments, ornaments and collyrium in my eyes. How sorrowful, sorrowful, I am. O, when will my love come home? I seek refuge with chaste brides and place my head on their feet. O, chaste brides unite me with my love. O, when will he visit my home? Listen my spouse, tell me the way to meet my beloved.
5th (**830**/5/2701)

Chopping off my head, I will place it under the feet of the one who causes me to meet my Lord God and unites me with his society.
4th (**836**/5/2721)

As the shell-duck craves for the sun, so thirsts Nanak for the feet of the Lord.
5th (**838**/5/2729)

My mind is in love. When shall I meet with my perfect groom through fortunate destiny? O my spouse, so counsel me that I may

obtain the Lord of the universe and be absorbed in him ... Prays Nanak, have mercy on me and attach me to the skirts of thy clothing, O Lord!
5th (**845**/5/2755-6)

Fondle me, O my beloved, for I behold thee amongst all. Meet me, that I may be emancipated. To dispel my spiritual darkness I always remember thee in my mind, like the female Ruddy-goose, who hopes to see the day dawn. Says Nanak, O my love, unite me with thyself. As the fish forgets not the water, so I forsake thee not.
5th (**847**/5/2762)

My boat filled with sins is tossed by the wind and I fear lest it should overturn.
Ist (**878**/6/2857)

Mercifully, save me, O master. I, the meek one, have sought thy protection.
4th (**881**/6/2868)

I look here and there and in ten different directions for him; my soul longs to meet my Lord. O my master, show mercy and unite me with thyself, supplicates Nanak.
5th (**928**/6/3026-7)

I ask for the society of saints. My master, bless me with it, so that I, a fool and an idiot, may also be saved. O God, the life of the world, I have sought thy protection. Shower thy mercy and

compassion on me and save me now.
4th (**975**/6/3197-8)

O Lord, thou art the cherisher of those, who seek refuge in thee. Save me, a great sinner.
4th (**976**/6/3200)

Shower thy benediction on me, O Lord, and save me, as thou didst save *Draupadi* from shame, when she was seized and brought to court by miscreants. I am a beggar and a serf at thy door, O my beloved, and I ask for a boon from thee. Show mercy to me.
4th (**982**/6/3220)

Save, save, save thou me, O my master and rescue me by showering thy benedictions on me.
4th (**983**/6/3224)

O, my lofty and inaccessible Lord God, the enemy of ego. Thy slave has sought thy protection. Pull me out of the arduous and dreadful ocean of the world.
5th (**988**/6/3237-8)

The Guru is the beneficent giver and I ask for this boon from the Guru, that he may unite me with my Lord, from whom I am separated since long ago. This alone is the greatest desire of my heart and body.
4th (**996**/6/3265)

Within my mind is the love of my beloved. How can I meet my

God, the friend that I may blend with him.
4th (**996**/6/3265)

What sins of mine should I narrate? I am intoxicated with the false love of the world. Nanak has come to God's sanctuary and refuge. O Lord, stretch out thine arms and take me into thy embrace.
5th (**999**/6/3273-4)

Glory is in the hands of my Lord. My hearty yearning is that thou shouldst unite me with thyself.
Ist (**1012**/6/3316)

Apart from God, I have no other prop or support. O my creator Lord, save me, the meek one. (*Note: should be "the dishonoured one" as in next couplet*).

If it pleases thee, O Lord, bless the dishonoured one with honour.
4th (**1071**/6/3522)

I know nothing of thy service and knowledge; my master, take thou pity on me, a mere worm. Blend me, the meritless one, with thyself, O Lord. Shower thy benediction on me and yoke me to thy service.
5th (**1078**/6/3546)

O Lord of compassion, the beneficent one, bless me with a vision of thyself and grant me understanding, that I may obtain salvation.
Ist (**1109**/7/3652)

Through my sins, I have wandered in various species and now have sought refuge in thee, O Lord. Take pity on me, O master and save me.
4th (**1114**/7/3669)

My Lord, pull me out of the love of sins and attach my mind to the society of saints. Thirsty, like the pied cuckoo thirsting for the raindrops, how can I live without God and how can I endure the pangs of separation. Slave Nanak, makes supplication: how can my life linger on without thee, O my God?
5th (**1120**/7/3687)

I am low and foolish like an exceedingly heavy clod of clay. My Lord God, show me mercy and unite me with thyself.
4th (**1178**/7/3883)

O Lord, thou art merciful to the meek and the destroyer of sorrow. Pull me, like a sinking stone out of the ocean of the world.
4th (**1179**/7/3886-7)

Says Nanak, I have fallen at thy door, O Lord. Save me, the stupid and ignorant one.
5th (**1186**/7/3908)

The whole world is diseased, for whom should I seek and search to cure me?
Ist (**1189**/7/3920)

Let some saint, God's holy man and my beloved holy man come and show me the way to my God.

Then I would rub, wash and bathe the feet of that man.
4th (**1201/7/3959**)

Despite my efforts this soul is not comforted. Is there any saint, who can help me to meet my groom? Worship, penance, self-control and alms sacrifice I shall do for my Lord. To him I dedicate all my comforts and my abode as well. I am devoted unto that saint who makes me see, even for an instant the vision of my beloved spouse.
5th (**1207/7/3977-8**)

I make supplication before my beloved Guru, that he may unite me with God, my spouse.
Ist (**1254/7/4137**)

O my omnipotent, unfathomable and omnipresent Lord, show mercy unto me. Ferry me across the very terrible blind well of the world, says Nanak.
5th (**1273/7/4198**)

O fearless, immaculate Lord, the man-lion, save me, a sinner and a stone.
4th (**1296/8/4277**)

O Lord, I seek refuge at thy feet. Save me from worldly love, ego, guile and doubt and cut the fetters from my feet. My master, I am being drowned in the world ocean.
5th (**1301/8/4293**)

I am filthy, stone-hearted, deceitful and lustful. As thou deemest fit, so save me, O my Lord ... Casting thy eye of grace upon me, O Lord, pull Nanak out of an awfully dark ditch.
5th (**1301/8/4295**)

If someone were to show me the way and path of the Lord, tell me, tell me, what should I give him? I would surrender, offer and dedicate my whole body and soul to him. Let someone unite me with my Lord.
4th (**1320/8/4356**)

O, Lord and master, the saviour of slave Nanak, save me, a sinking stone.
4th (**1320/8/4357**)

My Lord, show such mercy to me, that my sins may be burnt away in an instant.
4th (**1325/8/4374**)

Within me the powerful fire of sin is strongly raging. O my Lord, bless me with the icy-cold word of the Guru, that it may be quenched.
4th (**1325-6/8/4375**)

Prays Nanak, O Lord God, the man lion, I have sought thy protection, save me, save me.
5th (**1358/8/4482**)

I do not possess humility, compassion and piety, but I have sought thy refuge, O giver of spiritual life. God, the Lord of wealth, is omnipotent and able to

do everything. O master of
Nanak, save him by thy mercy.
5th (**1387/8/4579**)

O my illustrious God, the Lord of
Lakhshmi and the master of all,
slave Nanak has sought thy
refuge. Shower thy benediction
on him and save him now.
5th (**1388/8/4583**)

O Lord, I commit many sins, of
which there is no limit. O God,
mercifully pardon me; I am a
sinner and a great offender.
3rd (**1416/8/4680**)

O God, bless me with the dust of
the feet of the Guru's disciples,
that I, a sinner, may also be
emancipated.
4th (**1424/8/4708**)

I have grown weary of making
many efforts, but my mind's ego is
not effaced. I am engrossed in
evil intentions, says Nanak; save
me, O save me, my illustrious
Lord.
9th (**1428/8/4720**)

9

HINDUISM IN THE HOLY GRANTH

Introduction

A. Hindu Influence

1. Hindu myths in the Granth

2. Prayers directed to God through Hindu gods and Hindu names for God

A. The Break with Hinduism

Introduction

1. Rejection of Idol Worship

2. Rejection of bathing at Hindu pilgrimage places

3. Rejection of Hindu ritualism, fasting and asceticism

4. Rejection of Hindu gods in favour of the one and only God

5. Rejection of Pandits, Vedas and Puranas

6. Rejection of the Hindu caste system

7. Non-vegetarianism in the Granth

Introduction

It is no wonder that Hinduism forms the major portion of the Sri Guru Granth Sahib, since Sikhism is deeply rooted in Hinduism. Hindu philosophy and its terminology forms the basis of Sikh philosophy. Its concept of God, karma, maya, transmigration, samsara, sin and salvation is essentially the same. It was only with the creation of the khalsa panth by the tenth Guru, Govind Singh, that a marked outward difference between Hindus and Sikhs became apparent with the usage of the five K's by the Sikhs. Although the first Guru, Nanak, and the fifth Guru, Arjan Dev, had rejected Hindu rituals and pilgrimages in favour of the Name and the Guru, Hinduism still remained the core of Sikhism, as it depended on Hindu terminology to expound and ex-plain its new faith to the world. Some Sikh denominations, like Nirankaris and Namdharis, are deeply immersed in Hindu phil-osophy and are experts at expounding Sikhism in terms of Vedantic philosophy.

In summary we can safely say that the Granth is full of Hindu ref-erences, images and expressions, without which Sikhism would find it hard to express its religious philosophy to the world.

A. Hindu Influence

1. Hindu myths in The Granth

A separate book could be written about the references to Hindu myths, as there is an inexhaustible store of Hindu myths in the Holy Granth. Unfortunately we do not have the space to list all and will have to be content with a few selections.

The Guru is Shiva, the Guru is Vishnu and Brahma, the Guru is Shiva's consort Parvati, Vishnu's consort Lakshmi, and Brahma's consort Saraswati.
Ist (2/I/4)

The mythical bull is piety, the offspring of compassion, which is patiently holding the earth in order.
Ist (3/I/9)

How much is the load on the bull? If someone understands this, he becomes a true man.
Ist (3/I/9)

The unique, divine mother, master, formulating a plan of propagation, installed three approved disciples. The world's creator, Brahma, the steward who gives sustenance, Vishnu, and the one who has the disposition of destroying, Shiva.
Ist (6/7/1/22)

A good many are winds, waters and fires and a good many are Krishnas and Shivas. There are many Brahmas, who are fashioning forms and many beauties, colours and raiment.
Ist (**7/1/24**)

Countless are the earths and mountains for doing virtuous deeds and others without number are Dhruvas, instruction receivers. Countless are Indras, moons and suns, countless are universes and countless are countries.
Ist (**7/1/25**)

Wind, water and fire and righteous justice, sing thy praises at thy door.
Chitra Gupta, the recording angels, who know how to write as adjudicated by the righteous judge on the basis of inscribed writ, sing hymns to thee.
Shiva, Brahma and the goddess ever beautiful as adorned by thee, sing to thee.
Indra seated on his throne with deities at thy gate, sings to thee.
In meditative mood the perfect persons sing of thee and the saints in their contemplation sing as well. The chaste, the true and the patient sing thy praises and the dauntless warriors admire thee.
The scholars (pandits), the readers of the Vedas of all the ages, together with the seven supreme sages exalt thee.
The captivating she seraphs, who beguile hearts in paradise, this world and the nether regions, sing to thee.

The fourteen invaluable objects created by thee, together with the sixty-eight places of pilgrimage, sing hymns to thee.
Ist (**8/9/1/2829**)

From out of the ocean came the jewel, when the mountain of gold was used as a churning staff. The gods appointed the sixty-eight places of pilgrimage, where festivals are celebrated and hymns are recited.
Ist (**150/1/501**)

Brahma, the granter of boons, went with his progeny into the lotus tube to ascertain the world's extent. Proceeding further he could not find its limits. What glory was obtained by killing Kans? The ocean of milk was churned and gems were produced and brought forth. The gods and demons, etc. indignantly roared, "We have done this".
Ist (**350/3/1168**)

The Lord killed wicked Harnakshyapa and saved Prahlad.
4th (**451/3/1487**)

In the time of Yajur Veda, Krishna of the Yadav tribe seduced Chanderawati by force. He brought the elysian tree for his milk-maid and revelled in Brindaban.
Ist (**470/3/1551**)

Creating Brahma, Vishnu and Shiva with three qualities, God put them to work.
3rd (**509/3/1677**)

The elephant's fear departed in an instant, as soon as he uttered the Lord's name ... Listening to Narad's instruction the child Dhruva got absorbed in meditation.
9th (**830/5/2703**)

With the award of a punishment of a thousand wombs, Indra did weep.
Paras Ram returned home crying. Ajai wailed, when made to eat the dung he gave in charity, such is the punishment meted out in God's court.
Rama wept when he was exiled and got separated from Sita and Laxman.
Ten-headed Ravan, who took away Sita with the beat of a tambourine, wept when he lost Ceylon.
The Pandavas, whose master lived with them, became servants and wailed.
Ist (**953/4/6/3124**)

Show me thy blessing, O Lord and save me, as thou O Lord God didst save Draupadi from shame, when she was seized and brought to court by miscreants.
4th (**982/6/3220**)

Prahlad, thy slave, was caught by Harnakhsh. Thou didst save and

emancipate him, O Lord!
4th (**984/6/3225**)

The five year old orphan boy Dhruva became eternal and

motionless by meditating on his God.
For the love of his son, Ajamal called upon the Lord, who smote and drove away death's messengers. Within his mind the great elephant remembered God just for a moment and was saved.
The Lord preserved saint Prahlad and tore Harnakhsh with his nails. Bidar, the son of a maidservant, was sanctified and his entire lineage became illustrious.
5th (**999/6/3273**)

All the gods made obeisance unto the goddess of wealth saying: "O mother, let this horrible man-lion form disappear." Lakhshmi was terrified and could not go near. Saint Prahlad came and fell at the Lord's feet.
3rd (**1154/7/3801**)

He created millions of incarnations of Vishnu. He created and destroyed millions of Shivas.
He employed myriads of Brahmas to create the universe. Such is the Lord, millions of Lakhshmis are his handmaids and myriads of beings are his couches ... Millions of Indras stand at his door.
5th (**1156/7/3807**)

Ajamal was delivered uttering the Lord's name but once.
Balmik obtained the society of saints. Without hesitation the Lord met Dhruva. By uttering the Lord's name like her parrot, the prostitute was emancipated. The

great elephant remembered God and he delivered him.
5th (**1192**/7/3929)

The hunter, who struck Krishna with an arrow was delivered. Placing his foot on the thumb, the hunchback was saved. Bider was redeemed throught the servant's sentiments.
5th (**1192**/7/3929)

Bhagirath, the penitent, brought down the Ganges and Shiva established Kedar Nath.
4th (**1263**/7/4166)

Krishna grazed cows in Banaras. Through the touch of the Lord's slaves places attained glory.
4th (**1263**/7/4166)

Whosoever meditates on him is emancipated and merges in the Lord like Dhruva and Prahlad.
*4th (***1308**/9/8/4319)

Brahma, the son of a lotus and Vyas, the son of a fish, practised austerities and were worshipped.
4th (**1309**/8/4319)

King Janak while sitting on his throne took the dust off the feet of the nine sages and applied it to his forehead.
*4th (***1309**/8/4320)

The Serpent King utters the Lord's name with thousands of his hoods, but by so uttering his name he cannot find out the Lord's limits.
4th (**1309**/8/4320/1)

Krishna hugged Bidar to his heart and bosom, though he was an untouchable lad, the son of a maidservant.
*4*th (**1309**/8 4321)

Brahma, Shiva, adepts, silent sages and Indra beg for the gift of meditating on the Lord and praising him. The yogis, divines, men of reflection and the thousand-hooded serpent, all meditate on the playful Lord.
5th (**1322**/8/4361)

2. Prayers directed to God through Hindu gods and Hindu names for God

All the prayers of the Gurus are directed to the transcendent creator, known as **agam** *(inaccessible)*, **agochar** *(incomprehensible) and* **apaar** *(boundless), but any name for God may be used. Some prayers are addressed through Brahma or Paar Brahm, through Hindu incarnations, or through other names.*

Prayers are directed to Hindu gods, incarnations of Vishnu, such as Ram, also called Banvali (forest dweller), Krishna, also called by other names such as, Madho, Murari, Mohan (beloved enchanter), and Nar-Hare (the lion-man incarnation). Apart from these incarnations other names for Hindu gods have been used, such as Hari (translated as Lord or God), Brahma and Paar Brahm (translated as merciful and transcendent Lord or supreme Lord), Thakur (translated as the Lord), Govind (translated as world cherisher and Lord master, world Lord, master of the universe, etc), Jagan Nath (translated as Lord of the world and king of creation), and Jagdish (literally Lord of the world, translated as Lord of the universe, master of the universe, etc).

Prayers Addressed to Hari

There are hundreds of prayers; we will only give a few. "Hari" is translated by Manmohan Singh as "Lord" or "God".

O <u>God</u>, cause me to meet the society of saints and true persons.
4th (**96**/1/320)

My soul craves and my mind is thirsty for a sight of <u>God</u>, O Nanak!
5th (**133/134**/1/441-2)

O <u>Lord</u>, grant me a vision of thee. My hope is in thee.
4th (**164**/2/550)

The longing for <u>God</u> is ever within my heart and mind, O <u>God</u>! How shall I see thee?
4th (**167**/2/558)

Though I am without virtue, I make this supplication: O sovereign <u>Lord</u>, bless me with a sight of thee.
5th (**241**/2/799)

By thy grace, O <u>Lord</u>, I ask for thy name.
5th (**457**/3/1508)

In thought, word and deed I have not sung <u>God's</u> praises; this anxiety haunts my mind.
9th (**685**/4/2242)

I surrender my wealth, riches and property to him, who may unite me with God, my friend.
4th (**719**/4/2349)

O my life, let any comrade or mate of mine come and unite me with my Lord and master.
4th (**538**/4/1769)

Save, save me, O God, I am a worm slave of thine. I have sought thy protection, O Lord, my nourisher.
4th (**731**/5/2386)

O Lord God, merciful to the meek and poor, unite me with the society of saints.
4th (**732**/5/2387)

I have obtained the wealth of the Lord God's name and serf Nanak utters the master's name under the Guru's instruction.
4th (**997**/6/3268)

Throughtout the eight watches Nanak sings thy praise, O God, and begs from thee the gift of thy name alone.
5th (**1302**/8/4297)

Prayers Directed to Ram

O, omnipresent Lord, show mercy to us, who on account of deeds alone are separated from thee, and unite us with thyself.
5th (**133**/1/440)

O, my master, I am silly, save me O, my Lord God.
4th (**166**/2/554)

I am ignorant, O my all-pervading God, do thou accomplish my salvation.
4th (**166**/2/555)

My omnipresent Lord, shatter my shackles of mammon and devote me to the service of thy home.
4th (**166**/7/2/557)

Mother, O my mother, tell me of my beloved Lord.
4th (**369**/3/1230)

Within my mind I meditate on the Lord's name.
5th (**405**/3/1345)

I make efforts to meet my God but no effort of mine works.
5th (**542**/4/1771)

But the mind's fire is never quenched without the Lord's re-fuge.
5th (**545**/4/1793)

Hearken thou to my supplications O, my Lord and master. I am full of millions of sins, nevertheless I am a slave of thine.
5th (**547**/4/1798)

Show mercy, O God, show mercy, and save me by thy grace.
5th (**575**/4/1888)

In this age emancipation is obtained only through the Lord's name.
1st (**768/5/2511**)

I am low and the Lord is very high. How can I meet with him?
3rd (**772/5/2515**)

Bless thou me with the capital and wealth of the Lord's name, wherewith thirst and hunger are all effaced.
4th (**983/6/3222-3**)

Show thou mercy unto Nanak and make me meet the Guru. Contemplating my Lord, my soul is comforted.
4th (**983/6/3222**)

Prayers Addressed to Brahma and Paar Brahm

O, my strong-armed, powerful Lord, the ocean of peace, I am falling into the pit, take me by thy hand.
5th (**203/2/674**)

Pardon me, O supreme Lord and master. Nanak is ever a sacrifice unto thee.
5th (**403/3/1338**)

Be merciful, O my transcendent Lord, show mercy unto me, O God, the enemy of pride.
5th (**431/3/1422**)

O, transcendent Lord, my master, take pity on me and free me from these bonds.
5th (**680/4/2230**)

May I meet some such saint of the Lord creator, who is imbued with the supreme Lord's love. He shall eradicate the fifth of the intellect of my mind.
5th (**687/4/2248**)

Guru Nanak has met his transcendent Lord and is a sacrifice unto his feet.
5th (**747/5/2434**)

My mind wanders and wobbles and is not stable. It knows not the state of the supreme Lord.
5th (**1387/8/4579**)

Prayers Addressed to Thakur

Nanak is under thy protection, O Lord! Thy servant has come and fallen at thy door.
5th (**241/2/799**)

O, Lord, I am thy serf. I am without merit, no merit do I possess.
5th (**262/2/868**)

O, my Lord, mercifully preserve me.
5th (**495/3/1633**)

Is there any such saint, who may meet me, shake off all my anxiety

and enshrine within me love for my Lord?
5th (**687**/4/2248)

Have mercy on me, O my master and save me, I am unfortunate, lowly and a mere stone.
4th (**799**/5/2603)

The imperishable Lord has no form or outline, nor is he made of five elements.
5th (**816**/5/2658)

The glories are in the hand of my Lord.
1st (**1012**/6/3316)

My Lord show thou such mercy unto me that my sins be burnt away in an instant.
4th (**1325**/8/4374)

Prayers Addressed to Govind

Prays Nanak, take pity on me, O thou world cherisher, the master of the universe and the Lord of wealth.
5th (**248**/2/822)

On meeting the saintly persons, O my God, I have found my Lord and master, friend and comrade.
4th (**174**/2/580)

Meet me, O my Lord of the world, bestow on me thy name.
5th (**240**/2/793)

Beseeches Nanak, O God, the master of the universe and merciful to the meek, stretch out thy hand and redeem me.
5th (**546**/4/1797)

O God, the Lord of the world and destroyer of pain, I seek the refuge of thy feet, bless me, thy serf, with thy name.
5th (**683**/4/2236)

I serve my Guru, fall at his feet and say, pray show me the way to my master, the Lord of the world.
1st (**687**/4/2247)

Hide my faults, O my Guru-God, I a sinner have sought the refuge of thy feet.
5th (**828**/5/2694)

My soul thirsts for thy love and for a vision of thee; O Lord of the universe fulfil this desire of mine.
5th (**838**/5/2728)

O, my mate, so counsel thou me that I may attain to the Lord of the universe and be easily absorbed in him.
5th (**845**/5/2755)

Prayers Addressed to Gopal

Give me the support of thy hand, O Lord, the world cherisher and take me out of the pit.
5th (**203**/2/675)

Prays Nanak, take pity on me, O thou world cherisher, the master of the universe and the Lord of wealth.
5th (**248/2/822**)

Merciful master, save me, I have sought thy protection; O cherisher of the world, Nanak is a child of thine.
5th (**260/2/863**)

Thirsty with desire I wander thinking when I shall behold my Lord. O Nanak, is there any friendly holy man who may unite me with my master?
5th (**928/6/3026**)

O Lord, I sought thy refuge, save thou my honour and bless me with thy true name.
1st (**1274/7/4202**)

O Lord, I seek the refuge of thy feet.
5th (**1301/8/4293**)

O, great Lord, the world cherisher, Nanak thy child is drowning in the dreadful ocean of poison, mercifully save him.
4th (**1335/8/4407**)

Prayers Addressed to Murari

Be merciful, O my transcendent Lord. Show mercy unto me O God, the enemy of pride.
5th (**431/3/1422**)

O God, the enemy of pride, save me, I am lost in the love of worldly valuables.
5th (**547/4/1799**)

Now I have taken the protection of the Lord, the enemy of pride, and have found all comforts in God's name.
5th (**458/3/1509**)

O my lofty and inaccessible Lord God, the enemy of ego, thy slave has sought thy protection; Pull me out of the arduous and dreadful world ocean.
5th (**988/6/3237/8**)

Prayers Addressed to Nar-Hare (Lion Man)

O fearless, immaculate Lord, the man-lion, save thou me, the sinner and the stone.
4th (**1296/8/4277**)

Prays Nanak, O Lord God, the man-lion, I have sought thy protection, save me, save me.
5th (**1358/8/4482**)

Prayers Addressed to Jagan Nath

O Lord of the world show mercy to me and make me thy slave, the slave of thy slaves.
4th (**696/4/2277**)

O God, the king of creation, save me by thy grace.
4th (**1296/8/4278**)

Prayers Addressed to Jagdish

Without the Lord of the universe, none can save mortals.
1st (**225**/2/743)

My supreme Lord is the master of the universe and the Lord of the world. O God, the king of creation, save me by thy grace.
4th (**1296**/8/4278)

Prayers Addressed to Madho

Prays Nanak, take pity on me, O thou world cherisher, the master of the universe and Lord of wealth.
5th (**248**/2/822)

Prayers Addressed to Banvali (the forest dweller)

To repeat the Lord God's name is the yearning I long for, O God, the forest dweller, have mercy on me.
4th (**668**/4/2189)

Prayers Addressed to Mohan

I go searching for that enticing sweet beloved of mine.
5th (**703**/4/2299)

Mention of Hindu Yugas

In the first true age, the Town of Truth was inhabited. In the Treta-age there was some falling off. In Duaper only half the truth remained. In the dark age only one foot remained and then the one Lord was revealed by the Guru.
5th (**886**/6/2884)

B. The Break with Hinduism

Introduction

Although Sikhs make use of Hindu terms, expressions and concepts, such as Brahman, maya, karma, samsara, transmigration, sin and salvation in their presentation of Sikhism to the world, yet Sikhism has a separate identity and Sikhism is not Hinduism. It has completely broken with Hinduism. The break was slow and gradual beginning with Guru Nanak, who reacted against Brahmanism and the ritualism and corruption which was found at pilgrimage places. But at the time of Guru Arjan, the fifth Guru, the division became more open and noticeable with the institution of Sikhism's community kitchen called the *Langar*, its own esteemed book called the Adi Granth Sahib and with its separate monotheistic creed deeply rooted in the sacrifices and martyrdoms of some of their Gurus. The break with Hinduism became final and permanent with the creation of the *Khalsa* (the pure ones) by the tenth and last Guru. From then on the Granth was to lead them spiritually and the *Khalsa* or the *Panth* was to lead the Sikh community politically by demo-cratic means. In order to achieve this the Gurus had to get rid of Hindu idol worship, pilgrimage to holy places, the caste system and Hindu rituals, in favour of the Guru and the Name. The reading of the Vedas, penance and self mortification and visiting Hindu pilgrimage sites was discarded in favour of the Guru-God and the Name. The uttering of the Name was made meritorious and carried the merit of visiting all sixty-eight Hindu holy places, as we will see in detail from the Granth.

1. Rejection of idol worship

The Hindus have forgotten the primal Lord and are going the wrong way. As Narad instructed so worship they idols. They are blind, dumb and the blindest of the blind. The ignorant fools take stones and worship them. When those stones themselves sink; how will they ferry thee across?
*I*st (**556**/4/1830)

Worshipping goddesses and gods, O brother! What can they give him? The stone gods are washed with water, O brother! But they themselves sink in water.
*I*st (**636**/4/2090)

The Hindus die worshipping, worshipping the idols and the Muslims die bowing their heads. The former burn the dead and the latter bury them. None of the two finds the real state, O Lord!
*I*st (**654**/4/2146)

They who say the stone is god, in vain is their service. He who falls at the feet of the stone, vain goes his labour. The stone speaks not nor gives anything. In vain are the ceremonies of the idolator and fruitless is his service.
5th (**1160**/7/3820)

In thy house thou keepest the idol god, with all other gods. Thou, O Pandit, washest it and worshippest it. Thou offerest it saffron, sandal and flowers. Falling at its feet, thou greatly propitiatest it. Begging from men, thou (O god) wearest (clothes) and eatest (food). For thy dark deeds thou shalt receive unforseen punishment. The idol gives not to the hungry and saves not the dying.
*I*st (**1240**/1/7/4090)

They worship the lifeless stones and adore tombs. Their service all goes in vain.
4th (**1264**/7/4169)

2. Rejection of bathing at Hindu pilgrimage places

Bathing at the sixty-eight holy places was rejected in favour of the Guru and the name. However, the Hindu pilgrimage places were accepted as meritorious. The service of a true guru and utterance of the name could earn a devotee the merit of sixty-eight holy places, without ever visiting a bathing Ghat. This was the real point of the shift from taking holy dips in the sixty-eight holy centres of Hinduism.

To take pity on the sentient beings is more acceptable than bathing at sixty-eight places of pilgrimage and giving all alms. He on whom God mercifully bestows this virtue is a wise man.
5th (**136**/I/449)

If there be a pure water tank in front, then the filth is washed off. By bathing in the pond, still more filth attaches to the man. The perfect place of pilgrimage is the true Guru, who night and day meditates on the name of Lord God.
4th (**140**/I/463)

He who bathes at places of pilgrimage and wanders over the earth, finds no place of rest hereafter.
5th (**216**/2/714)

The desires of man's mind, ego and self conceit are not removed by leaving the body at a place of pilgrimage.
5th (**265**/2/881)

Millions of baths and ablutions at the holy places fill mortals with faith in this dark age.
5th (**747**/5/2436)

Men of evil minds and thievish bodies go to bathe at the pilgrim stations. The one part of their bodily filth is washed off by bathing, but they contract two more parts of mental filth.
*I*st (**789**/5/2570/1)

The gourd is externally washed, but within it is pure poison. The saint is well off without bathing. A thief is always a thief whether he bathes or not.
*I*st (**789**/5/2571)

Celibacy, self-discipline and pilgrimages are the faith of those ages. In the dark age the glorification of the Lord's name is the only righteous deed.
3rd (**797**/5/2598)

The Ganges, the Jamna, the confluence of the three streams, seven oceans, charity, alms and worship are contained in the Lord's name. Nanak, in Magh, the ablution at the sixty-eight holy places is contained in the meditation of the supreme elixir of the Lord's name.
*I*st (**1109**/7/3653)

By roaming at pilgrimage stations man is not rid of his disease.
Ist (**1153**/7/3798)

He is pleased not by wandering naked at places of pilgrimages. Sitting outside alone in the wilderness he is not softened. O Nanak, if one utters the true name, the Lord is supremely pleased.
Ist (**1237**/7/4078)

Instead of sixty-eight holy places, bathe, O man, in the Lord's name.
4th (**1263**/7/4166)

The man who bathes in the ambrosial water of the divine knowledge, takes with him the merit of bathing at the sixty-eight holy places. No pilgrim station is equal to the Guru.
Ist (**1328**/9/8/4383)

All the virtuous deeds, religious acts, purifications, self-mortifications, devotions, austerities and pilgrimages at the holies, abide in the Lord's name. Nanak, if the true Guru is found, he unites man with the Lord and then sorrow, sin and death flee away.
Ist (**1332**/8/4396)

Hear thou, O man, singing the Lord's praise would earn thee the merit of bathing at the sixty-eight holy places.
4th (**1337**/8/4413)

The Ganges, the Jamna, the Godavari and the Saraswati crave for the dust of the saints' feet.

They say: "We are full of the filth of our sins, until we take a dip in the dust of the saints' feet, which washes away our filth." As many as are at the pilgrim stations established by the gods, so many are they who long for the dust of the saints' feet.
4th (**1263**/7/4166/7)

How can his praise be recounted, who constructed the tank by his efforts? The merits of sixty-eight holy places, alms, good actions and supremely pure deeds are obtained by bathing in this tank. (i.e. *Amritsar*).
5th (**784**/5/2552/3

The Fifth Guru's Complete Break With Hinduism and Islam

I practise neither fasting, nor observance of the month of Ramzan. I serve him alone, who will save me in the end.

The one Lord of the world is my God. He ministers justice to both Hindus and Muslims.

I go neither on pilgrimage to Mecca, nor to worship at the holy places. I serve only the one Lord and no other.

I perform not Hindu worship, nor do I offer Muslin prayer. Taking the one formless Lord into my mind, I make obeisance unto him there.

I am neither a Hindu nor a Muslim. My body and soul belong to him, who is called God of the Muslims and the Lord of the Hindus.
5th (**1136**/7/3738)

3. Rejection of Hindu ritualism, fasting and asceticism

Pilgrimage to shrines, fasting and cleanliness and self-mortification are not of any avail, nor are rituals, religious ceremonies and hollow adoration. Deliverance, O Nanak, is in devotional service of God, through duality the mortal is engrossed in worldliness.
*I*st (**75,76**/I/256)

The performance of recitation, penance, self-mortification and other rites is plundered near at hand. He who abides in fasting, daily ceremonies and austerities obtains not even a shell for them. Hereafter, the way is different, O brother. These are of no avail there.
5th (**216**/2/714)

Worship, fasting, frontal marks, ablutions, the bestowal of copious alms and charity, self-mortification and the utterance of sweet words - with none of these is the Lord pleased. Showy recitation, penance, wanderings across the earth, attachment to austerities with body outstretched following the path of the Yogis and Jains - by such means the Lord is not pleased.
5th (**674**/4/2208/9)

Through religious rites God cannot be won over.
*I*st (**355**/3/1184)

He practices inner-washing and breath control. My dear if by these methods the Lord is not found, as I have performed many such rituals. Man may remain mum, make his hands like a leaf plate and wander naked in the forest; he may visit river banks, shrines and the whole earth, but duality leaves him not.
5th (**641/2/4/2104**)

Even though man may give gratuitous feasts, make burnt offerings, offer alms, perform penance and worship and ever endure bodily pain and suffering, but without the Lord's name he does not obtain emancipation and the redeeming name, which one gathers by the Guru's grace.
*I*st (**1127/7/3709**)

The ascetic's staff, begging bowl, hair tuft, sacred thread, loin cloth, pilgrimage to the holy places and excessive wandering abroad, bring thee no peace. Without the Lord's name peace is not obtained. He who utters the Lord God's name swims across. Though man may weave his matted hair into a crown, apply ashes to his body and casting off his clothes make his body naked, yet without the Lord's name he is not satisfied. Bound by prenatal deeds, he assumes sectarian garb.
*I*st (**1127/7/3747**)

Through burnt offerings, gratuitous feasts, mechanical recitations, penances, all self-mortifications and living on the banks of rivers and at holy places, God is not found.
5th (**1139/7/3747**)

Though he may observe fasts and perform religious ceremonies day and night; though he may be a Qazi, a Mulla, or a Shaikh; though he may be a Yogi, a wandering sage, or a hermit with ochre-coloured dress; without knowing the Lord, all are bound down and driven along by Yama.
*I*st (**1168/7/3850**)

One is not emancipated by wandering, wearing ochre-coloured robes. Through great self-mortification no one obtains peace of mind.
3rd (**1176/7/3874**)

The banks of rivers, six rituals, matted hair, incense burning and mace bearing, these do not serve the purpose. By means of a myriad sorts of efforts, austerities, wanderings and utterance of various gospels, the Lord's limits and seat cannot be found. I have given thought to all other ways, but peace lies in the name's meditation alone, O Nanak.
5th (**1306/8/4309**)

4. Rejection of Hindu gods in favour of the one and only God

In error are angelic persons, goddesses and gods. Lured by doubt are the men of miracles, strivers and the gods of creation.
5th (**258**/2/857)

Brahma, Vishnu and Shiva are afflicted with the ailment of three dispositions. They act in the spirit of I-amness.
4th (**735**/5/2398)

There have been ten incarnations, kings and forsakers like Shiva. They too found not thy limits, though some grew weary of smearing their body with ashes.
5th (**747**/5/2436)

Shiva, Brahma, demons and gods that are there, burn in the fire of death.
5th (**1267**/7/4179)

5. Rejection of Pandits, Vedas and Puranas

Tired of extensive reading, the pandits and men of silence, being attached to duality, have lost their honour.
3rd (**70**/1/237)

The Brahmins read books but do not understand their real meaning. They instruct others and walk away. They themselves trade in wealth.
Ist (**56**/1/190)

Many are the pandits and astrologers, who deliberate over the Vedas. They glorify disputes and strifes and through controversies continue in (the cycle of) coming and going.
Without the Guru, they cannot be absolved of their actions, however much they may talk, hear, preach and expound.
Ist (**56**/1/190)

By reading and studying the Brahmins set afoot controversies and without the Guru they go astray in scepticism.
They go round in the cycle of eighty-four lakh lives and without the name they do not obtain salvation. He is a Brahmin, who knows the Lord and is imbued with the love of God.
3rd (**67-8**/1/230)

The pandits and astrologers have grown weary of extensive reading

and the sectarians go astray in scepticism.
3rd (**68**/1/231)

The egocentric reads and is called a pandit, because of the love of another he suffers great pain. Intoxicated with evil passions he understands nothing and falls into the cycle of existence again and again.
The pandits read the Vedas but do not obtain God's nectar. Infatuated by mammon they enter into controversy. They who are ignorant are ever in darkness. Through the Guru men know God and sing his praises.
3rd (**128**/1/423)

The Vedas speak about the Lord but do not know his infinity. Not by studying but through understanding is the secret of the Lord to be found. Six are the creeds of the Shastras but rare is the person who merges in the true One through them.
Ist (**148**/1/493)

By reciting the four Vedas from memory, man does not attain to the Lord's presence hereafter. He who does not understand the one pure name only prates nonsense.
5th (**216**/2/714)

He instructs others, but understands not his own self. Such a Brahmin can in no way be emancipated.
O, silly Brahmin, meditate thou on

the Lord. He beholds and hears thee and abides with thee.
5th (**372**/23/1240)

Eighteen Puranas and four Vedas know not his secret, the true Guru has shown me the Lord, O Nanak.
Ist (**355**/3/1184)

Entanglements are the Vedas, religious discussion and the ego. By the entanglements of worldly love and sin, man is perishing.
Ist (**416**/3/1382)

Lakhs of comprehension and concentration and lakhs of readings of the Vedas and recitation of the Puranas are in vain. O Nanak, before the creator these acts of wisdom are false. True alone is the mark of his grace, who has made the world and has predestined the coming and going of all.
Ist (**467**/3/1541)

Brahma was born of the lotus of Vishnu's navel, attuning his voice he reads the Vedas with his mouth.
But the Lord's limit he could not find. He remained in the darkness of coming and going.
Ist (**489**/3/1615)

Gnosis is neither gained at Banaras, nor is the gnosis lost at Banaras. By meeting the true Guru wisdom is produced and then man obtains understanding.
3rd (**491**/3/1621)

Even though thou readest the Vedas for four ages, thou shalt not be freed of thy filthiness, O Pandit.
3rd (**647**/4/2124)

Reading and reciting the Vedas, Brahma grew weary, he did not find even a sesame seed's worth of God.
5th (**747**/5/2435)

By reading all the Vedas, the Smritis and the Shastras, and the religious books of the Muslims, salvation is not obtained.
5th (**747**/5/2437)

Utter thou the hymns of the Guru instead of the Vedas of Brahma and hold fast to this faith to dispel thy sins.
5th (**773**/5/2519)

Though man may reflect on the Smritis, the Shastras and the Vedas, it is meditation on the name, which alone emancipates him.
5th (**804**/5/2620)

In the end the true Guru said, "After me sing the praise of the pure Lord alone.
Call on only the Lord of the beautous hair, and read the Lord God's gospel instead of the Puranas.
Read only the Guru's gospel, hear only God's name. The Guru likes the Lord's love instead of barley rolls, food on leaves, Hindu

funeral rites, lamps and throwing bones into the Ganges.
3rd (**923**/6/3010)

The Shashtras and Vedas keep man bound to three modes of mammon and he does the blind deeds.
Ist (**1126**/7/3706)

Diseased are the six Shastras, several sectarians and many men of perseverance.

What can the poor Vedas and religious books do, when men understand not the one Lord?
Ist (**1153**/7/3798)

Though man may have with him eighteen Puranas written in his hand; though he may recite by heart four Vedas; though he may bathe on the festivals and give alms according to his caste ... But without knowing the Lord, all are bound down and driven along by Yama.
Ist (**1168**/7/3850)

If thou utterest the four Vedas with thy tongue and hearest the eighteen Puranas and six Shastras with thine ears, yet these equal not the divine melody of the Lord's name.
5th (**1229**/7/4051)

Thou keepest fasts, sayest vesper prayers, purifiest thyself and dost good deeds. Thou goest on pilgrimage in all directions and eatest nothing. Touching no one thou cookest thy food. Thou

makest a great display of inward washings. Thou burnest incense and lamps in the temples. All these equal not God's name.
5th (**1229**/7/4051-2)

Through wisdom, knowledge and yoga, he is not pleased.
*I*st (**1237**/7/4077)

The Brahmins read about strife, do the ceremonial deeds and daily routine and make others perform rituals.
*I*st (**1332**/8/4395)

Whosoever practices the inly-washing, making a furnace of the spinal chord, and engaging in inhalation, exhalation and suspension of breath (like a *yogi*), without the true Guru obtains not right understanding; and straying in doubt, he is drowned in death.
*I*st (**1343**/8/4431)

You read books, say vesper prayers, argue, worship stones and sit in trance like a crane.
With your mouth you utter falsehood like excellent ornaments and recite the triplet (the *Gayatri*) three times a day. Round your neck is a rosary, on your forehead the sacred mark and on your head a towel and you have two loin cloths. If you know the nature of the Lord, then you will find that all these beliefs and rites are vain.
*I*st (**1353**/8/4464)

The Brahmins have grown weary of performing *yajnas*, *Havans*, and pilgrimages to all the holies and of reading the Puranas. But they are not rid of the poison of the love of worldly riches and in egotism they continue coming and going.
3rd (**1417**/8/4684)

6. Rejection of the Hindu caste system

The rejection of the caste system by the Sikh Gurus was a revolutionary step, which deserves wholehearted appreciation. The ravages of the caste system under Hinduism had reduced low castes to despair. They were debarred from listening to the Scriptures and molten lead was supposed to be poured into the ears of a low caste Shudra, if he ever heard a mantra recited by a devotee desiring Moksha, as detailed in the famous Hindu book Manu-Smriti. Although the caste system had no place in Christianity and Islam had also done away with the caste system after Christ, it was a daunting task for the Sikh Gurus to allow all four castes to worship God through the Guru and the utterance of the name. It was further highlighted by the 10th Guru who created the Khalsa Panth. It is alleged that four out of the five Pyaras he selected were from the lowest stratas of the caste system. That was revolutionary during those days in a caste and superstition ridden society.

However, it was more difficult to get rid of the caste mentality. There are signs of this in the Granth Sahib, where unconciously people of menial birth are equated with evil or dishonour.

Nanak seeks the company of those who are of low caste among the lowly, nay rather the lowest of the low. Why should he (who has no desire to) rival the lofty?
Ist (**15**/1/48)

Call everyone exalted, no one appears to be base. The one Lord has fashioned the pots and one light pervades the three worlds.
Ist (**62**/1/212)

Preposterous is caste and vain its glory. The Lord alone gives shade to all beings.
Ist (**83**/1/280)

Man's body and caste shall not go to the next world, where he is called to account; there shall he be delivered by the practice of truth.
3rd (**112**/1/370)

What power has caste? Righteousness is to be desired. High caste pride is poison, by eating which man dies.
Ist (**142**/1/472)

What can cold do to fire and how can night affect the sun? What effect can darkness have on the moon? What effect has caste on air and water?
2nd (**150**/1/502)

He rises above all caste and caste marks, who under the Guru's instructions utters God's name, O Nanak.
5th (**259-60**/2/861)

Recognise the Lord's light within all and inquire not their caste, as there is no caste in the next world. *Ist* (**349**/3/1164)

Hereafter caste and beauty go not with man. As are the deeds he has done, so becomes he there. *3rd* (**363**/3/1210)

In the next world caste and power count not. Hereafter the mortal has to deal with new beings. *Ist* (**469**/3/1547)

Name and caste shall not go into the hereafter. The wayward person is consumed by anguish. *3rd* (**514**/3/1695)

The four castes of warriors, priests, farmers and menials are equal partners in divine instruction. *5th* (**747**/5/2437)

There are four castes of the literate, warriors, cultivators and menials and the four stages of life. He who meditates on the Lord is the most distinguished amongst men. *4th* (**861**/5/2803)

The warriors, the literate, the menials and the agriculturists all swim across only through the Lord's name. *5th* (**1001**/6/3281)

No one should be proud of his caste. He alone is a Brahmin who knows the Lord.

O stupid fool, be thou not proud of thy caste. From this pride many sins well up.
Everyone says there are four castes. But they all proceed from the Lord's seed.
The whole world is made out of one clay. But the potter has fashioned it into vessels of many sorts.
Merging together, the five elements make up the body's form. No one can say that any element is less in one and more in another.
Out of the four castes, whoever keeps awake is released from birth and death. *3rd* (**1128**/7/3710-11)

Caste or no caste, let everyone remember God; whoever remembers him is emancipated. *5th* (**1150**/7/3787)

I have lost my caste, birth and lineage, and sing the praise of my Lord God. *5th* (**1230**/7/4055)

If God's slave be in a high caste family, no one can utter his praises.
If there be a slave of the Lord in a low caste family, then Nanak will make footwear for him made of his own skin. *Ist* (**1256**/7/4143)

Neither the body, nor renown, nor caste accompanies mortal man into the hereafter. *Ist* (**1256-7**/7/4145)

Sovereignty, wealth, beauty, high caste and youth are the true robbers.
1st (**1288**/7/4252)

Whomsoever thou forgivest, he is blessed with high caste and honour.
1st (**1331**/8/4391)

The Lord asks not about a man's caste or birth, so find out the Lord's true home. The deeds which he does, that alone is man's caste, that is his glory.
1st (**1330**/8/4388)

Where man is called to account, there the body and caste do not accompany him.
3rd (**1346**/8/4442)

Evidence of Caste Mentality

Avarice is a dog, falsehood the sweeper and cheating the eating of carrion. Slandering others, amounts to putting other's filth in one's own mouth and the fire of wrath is a pariah.
1st (**15**/1/48)

The false one has no caste and honour. No one succeeds through falsehood.
1st (**23**/1/76)

He whom the Lord himself has put on the wrong track, has no caste and no honour.
5th (**42**/1/143)

The mortal acquires the father's caste only if the Guru being pleased shows favour unto him.
4th (**81-2**/1/275)

In the Lord God's name my faith lies and God's name is my caste and honour.
4th (**82**/1/277)

Evil intellect is the she-drummer, heartlessness is the butcheress, others' slander in the heart is a sweeperess and deceitful wrath is a pariah woman.
What does the drawing of lines avail thee when these four are seated with thee?
1st (**91**/1/305)

A low pariah woman becomes a high caste lady and a sweeperess is rendered sublime.
5th (**381**/3/1267)

The *Khatris'* way is the way of bravery, the way of the *Sudras* is the way of service of others.
2nd (**269**/3/1549)

The *Khatris* have abjured their religion and have taken to a foreign language.
The whole world has assumed the same caste and the ordinance of righteousness has lapsed.
1st (**663**/4/2173)

He is a swine, a dog, a donkey, a cat, a beast, a filthy one, a mean man and a pariah (low caste), who turns his face away from the Guru.
1st (**832**/5/2708)

They who are without the name, have no caste and no honour and no one even cares for their name.
Ist (**1188**/7/3915)

What can I say, when I myself am nothing? All my caste and honour are through thy name.
Ist (**1189**/7/3921)

However, the five pariahs thou has brought with thee. Leaving thy country thou wanderest abroad.
5th (**1348**/8/4448)

7. Non-vegetarianism in the Granth

However many grains of corn there may be, none is without life. In the first place there is life in the water, by which all are made green.
Ist (**472**/3/1560)

Animals are food for animals, such meat the Lord gives them. They whom he has created in the ocean, the Lord takes care of.
2nd (**955**/6/3130)

Man is first conceived in flesh and then abides in flesh.
When he comes to life, he obtains a mouth of flesh and his bones, skin and body are made of flesh.
When he is taken out of the womb of flesh, he has a mouthful of milk from teats of flesh.
His mouth is of flesh and his tongue is of flesh and his breath is in flesh.
When he grows up, he is married and brings a wife of flesh into his home.
Flesh is produced from flesh and all the relatives of man are made of flesh.
When man meets with the true Guru, he knows the Lord's will and then alone is he reformed.
Fools quarrel over flesh, and know not God's gnosis and meditation.
They know not what is called flesh and what is green, nor in what does sin consist.

It was the habit of the gods to kill a rhinoceros and perform sacred feasts after burnt offerings.

They who abandon meat and hold their nose when sitting near it, devour men at night.

They practise hypocrisy and make a show of it to men, but they know not the knowledge of God and meditation. Nanak, what can be said to the blind man? He cannot reply, nor does he understand what is said to him. He alone is blind who does blind deeds. He has no mental eyes.

They are produced from the blood of their mother and father, yet they eat not fish and flesh. When man and woman meet at night, there they co-habit with flesh.

From flesh we are conceived, from flesh we are born and we are the vessels of flesh. O Pandit, thou knowest not divine knowledge and meditation on the Lord and still thou callest thyself wise.

Thou deemest the external flesh bad and the internal flesh good. All creatures have sprung from flesh and the soul has taken its abode in flesh.

They, whose teacher is blind, eat what is uneatable and abandon and reject what is eatable. In flesh we are conceived, from flesh we are born and we are the vessels of flesh.

O Brahmin, thou knowest not divine knowledge and meditation on the Lord and yet thou callest thyself clever.

Flesh is allowed in the Puranas, flesh is allowed in the Muslim religious books and flesh has been used in the four ages.

Flesh adorns sacred feasts and marriage functions, with them flesh is associated. Women, men, kings, emperors spring from flesh. If thou seest them going to hell, then thou shouldst not accept their gifts in charity. See ye this injustice, that the giver goes to hell and the receiver to heaven.

*I*st (**1289**/7/4256-7-8)

10

MUSLIM AND SUFI INFLUENCE ON THE GURUS

Introduction

1. **The effect of the Muslim invasion of India**

2. **Sufi influence on the Gurus**

3. **Rejection of Islam, the Quran and the Semitic scriptures**

Introduction

A Word about Sufism

The Gurus in general and Guru Nanak in particular were greatly influenced by Sufism. A Sufi seeks to be one with the ultimate reality through love and utter devotion by becoming a Faqir and renouncing the world and its attractions, such as wealth, property and family. For a Sufi the world is a passing phase. Therefore worldly attachments must not come between him and his God. Through utter devotion to God, he establishes the relationship of lover and beloved between him and his God. God is the spouse and the Sufi is the wife. Their spiritual union is the highest state of ecstasy between lover and beloved. It is at this stage of spiritual union that the Sufi *Darwesh* or *Pir* merges with God and becomes one with him (*Hama'ous*). There are four stages to spiritual progress according to Sufism.

1. *Shariat* ... Rituals

2. *Tarikat* ... Adoration

3. *Marfat* ... Divine knowledge

4. *Hakikat* ... Reality

In the 4th stage a Sufi becomes one with reality and says "I am he". Compare this with Vedanta, where a Bhakta says "*Aham Brahm-Asmin*".

We can see the effect of Sufism on Guru Nanak, for example in the way he calls God his spouse, "*khasam*" (husband) and in the many hymns where he is pleading as a wife with his spouse (God) for vision and spiritual union. He also stresses the need for renunciation of the world, as we see from these two quotations:

Centering their attention on the husband (*khasam*) alone, those who meditate upon him, receive his grace descending on them and they become pleasing to his heart. Ist (**24**/1/81)

We can clearly see Sufi thought prevalent in the hymns of Guru Nanak and Guru Arjan Dev. Guru Nanak says, "Think not that the spouse is obtained by mere words." Ist (**24**/1/80)

We have to differentiate, however, between Sufi influence on the Gurus and the impact of Muslim religious practices on Hindus, which the Gurus reacted to and rejected.

The Adi Granth contains large sections of Sufism by Sufi saints such as Farid and Kabir etc. As our search is limited to the Gurus only, we will not be able to reproduce quotations from the Sufi Bani here.

1. The effect of the Muslim invasion of India

With the conquest of India by Babur and imposition of Zazia or the temple tax, the influence of Islam was felt all over India. This touched the heartstrings of Guru Nanak, who had witnessed great bloodshed inflicted by Babur. Guru Nanak felt outraged and even complained to God, saying:

Having conquered *Khurasan* Babar has terrified Hindustan. The creator takes no blame on himself and has sent the *Mughal* as death's messenger. So much beating was inflicted that people shrieked. Didst thou, O God, feel no compassion?
Thou, our maker, art the master of all. If a mighty man smites another mighty man, then the mind feels no anger. But if a powerful tiger falling on a helpless herd kills them, its master should take responsibility. The dogs have spoiled and laid waste the precious country. No one pays heed to the dead.
Ist (**360**/3/1200)

Guru Nanak further describes his frustration and disgust by saying:

He whom the creator destroys, he first deprives of virtue.
When they heard of the invasion of the emperor Babar, then millions of religious leaders failed to halt him. He burned houses, resting places and strong palaces. Having cut the princes into pieces, he caused their bodies to roll in the dust.
But no Mughal became blind and no (religious leader) wrought any miracle!
Ist (**417-418**/3/1385)

There raged a contest between the *Mughals* and the *Pathans* and the sword was used on the battlefield. The *Mughals* aimed and fired their guns and the *Pathans* attacked with their elephants. They whose fate had been decreed in God's court, must die, O my brother.
There were women who were Hindus, Muslims, Bhattis and Rajputs. The robes of some were torn from head to foot and some were hiding in the cremation ground. How did they, whose handsome husbands never came home, pass the night?
The creator of himself acts and causes others to act. To whom then should man go to wail?
Ist (**418**/3/1386)

The primal Lord is called Allah; the turn of the Muslim divines has come. Tax is levied on the temples of gods. Such a practice has come into vogue. The ablution-pots, calls for prayer and prayer carpets are seen everywhere and the Lord appears in the blue form. In every house all the persons say *'Mian';* your language has become different, O

man. If thou, O Lord wishest to appoint *Mir Babur* the king of the earth; what power have I to challenge it?
*I*st (**1191**/7/3926)

In the *Kalage* (dark age), the Quran has become the approved book. The Brahmins, the Hindu religious books and the Puranas are not esteemed. The merciful *Khuda* is now the Lord's name, O Nanak.
*I*st (**903**/6/2942)

In the dark age *Atharava Veda* became prominent and Allah became the name of God.
*I*st (**470**/3/1551)

Men then took the blue robes and dresses (and followed the Turks and the Pathans).
*I*st (**470**/3/1551)

Thou wearest a loin-cloth, puttest on a frontal mark, carriest a rosary and eatest the Muslim provisions. O brother, within thou performest worship, outside thou readest Muslim books and adoptest the Muhammedan (Turki) way of life.
*I*st (**471**/3/1556)

Wearing blue clothes, he becomes acceptable in the eyes of the Muslims. Taking bread from the Muslims he worships the Puranas. He eats the he-goat killed by uttering foreign words *(Halal)*.
He allows none to enter his cooking enclosure.
*I*st (**472**/3/1557)

The preceding quotations of Guru Nanak show that the influence of Islam on the Hindus was wide-ranging, covering their eating habits, dress, language and religious thought. Guru Nanak was against the Mughal conquest of India and the Islamisaton of India, yet he felt a great need to help both Hindus and Muslims to understand that Akaal Purukh, the eternal one, whom Hindus call Ram and Muslims call Allah Rahim, was the same. It was a great message for those turbulent times, a message of love, tolerance and humanity, which he carried wherever he went with his two disciples Bala and Mardana.

It shows a great spirit of tolerance on the part of the Gurus, that Muslim names for God were unreservedly used in the Bani (Granth), for example Allah, Maula, Saneen, Khuda, Rahim, Qadir, Karim. Persian and Arabic words were used repeatedly. Some of the Gurus were great scholars of Persian and Arabic. More than that they were well versed in the knowledge of Muslim scriptures and practices. Even the names of Muslim angels were no exception as is clear from the following stanzas:

The rebels of the Lord with outstanding debt against them, shall be called to account.
The death courier *Azrail* (angel of death) shall be appointed to punish them.
*I*st (**953**/6/3123)

They who commit sins are assuredly plundered. *Azrail*, the angel of death, seizes and tortures them to death.
5th (**1019**/6/3342)

2. Sufi influence on the Gurus

The Gurus were well versed in the Vedas and in Muslim and Semitic books (Quran and Kateb). Kateb means the Torah, the Zabur and the prophets (Old Testament) and the Injil (New Testament) as mentioned in the Quran. Though it is doubtful if the Gurus ever read the Bible as such, they certainly read the Quran, as appears from the passages in the Granth where the Gurus have interpreted Muslim tenets of faith and given them new meanings.

Guru Nanak's interpretation of Muslim tenets of faith

The scriptures *(Vedas)* say that by trying to find the limits of God, people have grown weary.
The Semitic (Muslim) scriptures say that there are eighteen thousand worlds, but in reality there is only one truth (that the Lord is limitless).
Ist (**5**/1/15)

Make pious deeds thy farm, make the Guru's word thy seed and ever irrigate it with the water of truth.
Ist (**24**/1/80)

Even though thou keepest thirty fasts and takest with the five comrades (i.e. the five prayers), beware lest the one who goes by

the name of Satan should undo thy merit.
Ist (**24**/1/81)

He is the master *(Maula)*, who has made the world blossom and made the universe verdant. Hail to the creator, who has kept in bondage the water and the land. Death, O *Maulvi*, death must come. All the same abide in the fear of the maker.
Ist (**24**/1/81)

If thou knowest the name of God, then alone art thou a Mullah or then alone art thou a *Qazi*.
Even though a man be very learned, none can stay here when his measure of life has been fullfilled.
He is the *Qazi* who has renounced self-conceit and made the name of God alone his support.
Thou recitest prayer five times a day and readest holy books (Semitic religious books) and the Quran. Says Nanak, the grave calls thee and now thy food and drink have come to an end.
Ist (**24**/1/82)

Allah is the unseen, inscrutable, inaccessible, omnipotent *(Qadir)* and bounteous *(Karim)* creator. The entire world is subject to coming and going. The merciful *(Rahim)* Lord alone is permanent.
Ist (**64**/1/219)

Make mercy thy mosque, faith thy prayer-mat, what is just and lawful thy Quran, modesty thy circumcision and civility thy fast.

So shalt thou be a Moslem. Make right conduct thy Mecca, truth thy spiritual guide and pious deeds thy creed and prayer.
Ist (**140**/1/466)

The rosary is that which is pleasing to him. Thus the Lord shall preserve thy honour, O Nanak.
Ist (**141**/1/466)

Nanak, what is right to another is (like eating) swine for a Musalman and cow for a Hindu.
The spiritual guide and the prophet shall stand surety only if man does not eat carrion.
By mere talk man does not go to heaven. Deliverance comes by the practice of truth alone.
By putting condiments in unlawful food, it does not become lawful. O Nanak from false talk only falsehood is obtained.
Ist (**141**/1/466-7)

There are five prayers, five times for prayers and the five have five names.
The first is truthfulness, the second honest earning, the third charity in God's name, the fourth is pure intent and the fifth the Lord's admiration and praise. Repeat the creed of good deeds and then call thyself a Moslem.
Ist (**141**/1/467)

To be called a Muslim is difficult. If one be really so, then he may get himself called a Muslim.
First, he ought to deem sweet the religion of the Lord's devotees

and have his pride of self effaced as with a scraper.
Becoming a true disciple of the faith of the prophet, let him put aside the illusion of death and life.
He should heartily submit to the Lord's will, worship the creator and efface his self-conceit.
Therefore, if he is merciful to all sentient beings, O Nanak, then alone shall he be called a Musalman.
Ist (**141**/1/468)

He who deems that both the ways lead to the one Lord shall be emancipated.
The utterer of lies shall burn to ashes, fallen in the blasphemer's hell.
In the whole world the most sanctified are they who remain absorbed in truth. By eradicating self-conceit man is exonerated in the Lord's court.
Ist (**141**/1/471)

The spiritual guides (*Pir*), prophets (*Paigumber*) and religious instructors (*Masaik*), seers (*Auliya*) and men of miracles meditate on thee. Like warp and woof, the formless Lord (*Mauliya*) is woven into all hearts.
5th (**518**/3/1708)

Hail, hail unto thee, O Lord, thou who has created the world, hast made us.
Thus hast made the ocean currents, the ocean, water pools, vegetation, clouds and mountains.

Whilst creating the creation, thou thyself standest amidst it, O Lord. Thou art all in all.
Ist (**788**/5/2568)

This great piece of Sufi teaching in Persian is by the learned 5th Guru:

Infusing his light into the dust, the Lord has made the universe and the world.
Sky, earth, trees and water are the Lord's creation.
O man, whatever the eye sees is perishable.
The world is an eater of carrion, neglectful of God, and avaricious.
Like a ghost and a beast, the world kills the forbidden and eats the carrion.
Restrain thy heart, otherwise the omnipotent Lord shall seize thee and punish thee in hell.
Patrons, dainties, brothers, courts, lands and houses - tell me, of what avail shall these be to thee when *Azrail*, death's messenger seizes thee?
My immaculate Lord (*Pak Allah*) knows thy condition.
O Nanak, utter thy prayer to pious persons, that they may lead thee to the right path.
5th (**723**/4/2360-1)

O creator, seeing thy providence, I have become thy lover.
Thou alone art my spiritual and temporal Lord. Thou, O God, art detached from the entire creation.

My compassionate God, thou thy-self art the master of beings and the Lord of the world.

Azrail, death's messenger, is the friend of mortals, who has thy support, O Lord.

All his sins are pardoned and thy slave sees thee.

All worldly things are for the present alone. True peace is in thy name, O Lord.

O, my wise king, I think of thee in my mind. O true sovereign, the releaser from bondage, love for thee abides in my mind and body.

The worth of seeing the Lord cannot be evaluated.

Thou art the immaculate cherisher. Thou thyself art the great and immeasurable Lord.

Assist me, O chivalrous Lord, for thou only art my creator Lord. By the power with which thou didst create the world, thou art Nanak's mainstay.

5th (**724**/4/2363-4)

The following passages are rich in Sufism and rich in Persian and Arabic vocabulary, as used by the 5th Guru Arjan Dev. Unfort-unately, the original poetry can-not be reproduced in English.

O, the slave of the boundless Lord God (Allah), renounce thou the thought of all worldly occupations.

Become thou the dust of the feet of the emancipated mortals and think thyself a traveller. Like this, O saint, thou shalt be approved at the Lord's door.

5th (**1083**/6/3564)

Make truth thy prayer (*Namaz*) and faith thy prayer-mat (*Mus-salla*). Still thy desire and over-come thy hope. Make thy body the mosque (*Masjid*), thy mind the priest (*Maulana*) and to be genuinely pure thy divine word (*Qalam*).

5th (**1083**/6/3564)

Make thou the practice of the name and religious conduct thy *'Shariat'*, the first stage of moral life. Make the search for God and abandonment of the world thy *'triquat'*, the second stage of the moral life. O holy man, make the silencing of the mind thy *'marfat'*, the third stage, and meeting with God thy *'Haqiqat'*, the fourth one by which thou shalt not die again.

5th (**1083**/6/3564-5)

Instead of reading the Quran and other religious books, practise thou in thy mind the restraint of the ten (sense-organs) from stray-ing into evil ways. Bind the five men or demons with faith, charity and contentment and thus shalt thou be accepted.

Make kindness thy 'Mecca' and the dust of the saints' feet thy 'fasting'. Deem the practice of the prophet's word as heaven. God alone is beauty, light and fragrance and meditation on the Lord is the sublime chamber of worship.

He alone is a 'Qazi' who practises truth. He alone is the pilgrim who has been to Mecca (Haji), who purifies his mind. He who banishes Satan is a 'Maulana' and he whose support is the Lord's praise is a saint (Darvesh).

At all times and all moments do thou remember in thy mind God, the creator. Make the subjugation of thy ten organs thy rosary for remembering God, and make good conduct and great self-restraint thy circumcision.

Know in thy mind that everything is but short-lived. Thy family, home and brothers are all entangle-lements. Kings, rulers and nobles are perishable. God's gate alone is the ever stable place.

The first prayer is the Lord's praise, the second contentment, the third humility and the fourth alms-giving. The fifth prayer is the restraint of the five desires in one place. These are the five exceed-ingly sublime times of prayer.

Make the knowledge that God is everywhere, thy daily worship. Make the abandonment of evil deeds the water-pot in thy hand. The knowledge that there is but one God is thy call to prayer and to be a good child of the Lord is thy trumpet.

Eat thou the food which is rightly earned. Wash away thy pollution in the river of thy mind. He who knows his Prophet is a man of paradise. Azrail, death's courier, will not goad him into hell.

Make good deeds thy body and faith thy bride. Revel thou in the true Lord's love and entertainment. Make pure what is impure. Deem the Lord's presence thy council. Let the complete body be the turban on thy head.

A Muslim is he who is kind-hearted. He ought to cleanse inner pollution from his mind. He should not draw near worldly pleasures and ought to be pure like a flower, like silk, clarified butter and a deer-skin.

He on whom is the grace and compassion of the merciful Lord is the manliest among men.

He alone is the Muslim preacher, the chief of sheiks, the pilgrim Mecca and the Lord's slave, on whom is the grace of God, the Man.

5th (1084/6/3566)

Power belongs to the omnipotent Lord and kindness to the kind master. Unfathomable are the praise and love of the merciful master. O Nanak, realise the true will of the true Lord and thou shalt be released from prison and shalt be freed.

5th (1084/6/3567)

In praise of God (Allah)

Excellent, excellent, excellent, excellent, excellent is thy name.
False, false, false, false is worldly
love.
Invaluable is the vision of thy
slaves, O infinite Lord.
Without the name, the whole
world is but ashes.
Wondrous is thy omnipotence and
praiseworthy are thy feet.
Priceless is thy praise, O my true
king.
The Lord's protection is the
support of the supportless.
Day and night I meditate on God,
the patron of the poor.
The Lord himself is merciful unto
Nanak.
May I not forget God (*Allah*),
who is my mind, my soul and my
very life.
5th (**1138**/7/3743-4)

A beautiful prayer of Guru Nanak in Persian

The great effulgence of the world
is but a passing show. My perverted intellect thinks not of the
grave.
I am but a lowly, humble peti-
tioner and thou, O Lord, art a
great river.
Bless me with one thing, thy
name. The other poisonous thing
pleases me not.
By thy skill, O Lord, thou hast
filled this fragile body as a bowl
with the water of life.

Through thy omnipotence, I have
become powerful.
Nanak is the inebriated dog at the
Lord's court; this inebriation of
his increases day by day.
This world is but fire and cool
alone is the Lord's (*Khuda*) name.
1st (**1291**/7/4262-3)

3. Rejection of Islam, the Quran and the semitic scriptures

The scriptures (Vedas) say one thing searching after God's limits and bounds, yet without success people have grown weary. The Semitic scriptures say that there are eighteen thousand worlds but in reality there is only one essence: that the Lord is limitless.
Ist (**5**/1/15)

The *Qazis*, the *Shaikhs* and the *Faqirs* in religious garb call themselves great, but through pride their bodies are in pain.
1st (**227**/2/749)

The Lord is beyond the Vedas and all the other religious books (*Kateb* or Semitic scriptures) of the world. Nanak's king is seen manifest everywhere.
5th (**397**/3/1317)

The Muslims praise Islamic law (*Shariat*). They read and reflect upon it. The Lord's servants are those who fall captive to see his sight.
Ist (**465**/3/1535)

Standing with the Vedas and the Semitic scriptures (*Kateb*) at thy door, mortals contemplate on thee.
5th (**518**/3/1707)

He has not mother, father, son and kinsman. He feels not lust and has no wife.
Ist (**597**/4/1962)

All the Vedas, the religious books of the Muslims, the Smritis and the Shastras, by reading these salvation is not achieved. He, who by the Guru's instruction utters the one name, gathers the pure glory.
5th (**747**/5/2437)

Thou art the master of hearts, the adjudicator of justice and more sacred than the Quran and other Semitic texts.
5th (**897**/6/2922)

The Vedas and Semitic texts know not the Lord's mystery. He has no mother, father, son and brother.
Ist (**1021**/6/3348)

The judge, the preacher, and the penitent shall all arise and depart. The spiritual leaders, the prophets and apostles, none of these shall remain stable. The fasting, the call to prayer, the prayers and the Muslim religious books, they shall all vanish without knowing the Lord.
5th (**1100**/6/3623)

Though he may be a *Qazi*, a *Mullah* or a *Shaikh*, though he may be a yogi, a wandering sage, or an hermit of ochre-colour dress ... But without knowing the Lord, all are bound down and driven along by *Yama*.
Ist (**1169**/7/3850)

If there be any other equal to thee,
O Lord, may I utter thy praises
before him. I praise thee before
thee, O Lord.
*I*st (**1242**/7/4095)

Rejection of Islam and Hinduism by the 5th Guru

I practise not fasting, nor observe
I the month of *Ramazan*.
I serve him alone, who will save
me in the end.
The one Lord of the world is my
Lord.
He ministers justice to both
Hindus and Muslims.
I go not on pilgrimage to Mecca,
nor do I worship at the holy
places.
I serve only the one Lord and not
any other.
I perform not Hindu worship, nor
do I offer Muslim prayer.
Taking the one formless Lord into
my mind, I make obeisance unto
him there.
I am neither a Hindu, nor a
Muslim.
My body and soul belong to him,
who is called God of the Muslims
and Lord of the Hindus.
5th (**1136**/7/3738-9)

INDEX

BIBLIOGRAPHY

The following is a brief selection of books aimed at providing an understanding of the Guru Granth Sahib in the context of the Sikh religion.

The Psalm of Peace: Teja Singh; Khalsa Brothers, Amritsar, 1937, frequently reprinted. Teja Singh was one of the great Sikh scholars. This is a translation with introduction of a composition used daily by individuals and groups of Sikhs in their meditations.

Sikhism: its Ideals and Institutions: Teja Singh; Orient Longmans, 1938, frequently reprinted. This brief collection of essays has greatly influenced Sikh thought and practice since its publication sixty years ago.

The Heritage of the Sikhs: Harbans Singh; Manohar, Delhi, 1994 edition. A readable survey by a scholar who was at the centre of Sikh affairs throughout his life until his death in 1998.

Berkeley Lectures on Sikhism: Harbans Singh; Manohar, 1995 edition. These constitute a brief introduction to Sikhism. Many western readers have found them very helpful.

The Encyclopaedia of Sikhism: Harbans Singh; Punjabi University, Patiala, 4 volumes 1992-1998. A supreme achievement which anyone with a serious interest in Sikh studies must possess.

The Name of my Beloved: Nikky Guninder Kaur Singh; HarperCollins, San Francisco and London, 1996. An anthology in modern English of the most important scriptural passages which Sikhs use daily and on important occasions such as weddings.

The Golden Temple: Patwant Singh; Times Book International, 1998. This lavishly illustrated book goes as near as any can to doing justice to one of the most beautiful buildings in the world.

Gurdwaras in India and Around the World: Patwant Singh; Himalayan Books, New Delhi, 1992. A similar study but, as the name implies, this time the canvas is broader.

Guru Nanak and the Sikh Religion: W H McLeod; Oxford University Press, 1969. A western approach to the historical Guru Nanak. Probably the finest analysis of Sikh theology/philosophy available in English.

The Sikhs: Their Religious Beliefs and Practices: W Owen Cole and Piara Singh Sambhi; Sussex Academic Press, 1995. Widely acknowledged as the most comprehensive modern introduction to Sikhism. Used in many high schools and universities.

Sikhism: W H McLeod; Penguin Books, 1997. A valuable introduction to the religion. Both this and Cole and Sambhi provide detailed annotated bibliographies which the reader who has come thus far can use to aid further exploration.